The New Decorating with Pictures

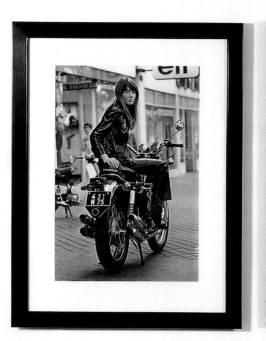

The New
Decorating with Pictures

Collecting Art and Photography and Displaying It in Your Home

  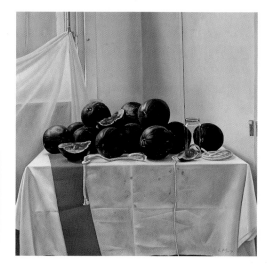

Stephanie Hoppen   Photography by Simon Upton

Bulfinch Press

New York • Boston

To my son, Michael, whose unerring eye and taste were both inspiring and challenging

Bulfinch Press

Time Warner Book Group
1271 Avenue of the Americas
New York, NY 10020
Visit our Web site at www.bulfinchpress.com

First United States Edition

First printed in Great Britain in 2004 by Jacqui Small, an imprint of Aurum Press Ltd.

ISBN 0-8212-2866-8

LCCN 2004102597

Design: Lisa Pettibone

PRINTED IN CHINA

page 1
Three "chicks" side by side. From left to right: Françoise Hardy by Reg Lancaster, 1969; Jane Birkin by Joseph McKeown, 1970; Marianne Faithfull by Hoare, 1950.

page 2
Fay Gold's family home is a magnificent showcase for her collection of contemporary art, sculpture, and furniture. This superb oil painting by Christopher Brown dominates one wall in the living area.

page 3
From left to right: "Facing the Horizon IV" by Marco Crivello; "Derby Spectator" by an unknown artist; "Watermelons" by Martin La Rosa.

this page
In Tim Hobby's elegant home, one's eye is immediately drawn to the beautiful panel with human figure by Todd Murphy. This dreamlike work is hauntingly beautiful and in total harmony with the room.

Contents

1 I have several collections of paintings in my bedroom. Here you can see a group of watercolors of children—mostly late-eighteenth and early-nineteenth century—with a pretty gilt frame above them. On either side of the window, Michael Houghton has hung mixed-media designs for ballet costumes by Yolanda Sonnabend. The Swedish oil over the bed is flanked with gilt mirrors. Scattered on every surface I have family photographs, usually framed in tortoiseshell.

A Passion for Pictures

I grew up in a home where pictures hung on all the walls of all the rooms. Oil paintings, both antique and modern, cohabited with watercolors and mirrors. Photographs of great-grandfathers with beards, top hats, or military uniforms stared out at us, and sets of Hogarth prints of London decked the walls of the staircases. Large hangings and embroideries were also present—my parents had eclectic tastes and it all was part of the tapestry of our lives.

It is hard for me to relate to empty walls, yet one sees them in certain modern magazines looking self-consciously barren. I wonder what it says about the owners of such walls? To me there is something so empty about a home without paintings, photographs, and suchlike. They are so very much the soul of a home. To say I hope this is a passing phase is an understatement. Like a woman's face, the walls of a house do not look good unadorned. They need something that adds warmth, personality, depth, interest, texture, and—most of all—soul, to the life and spirit of the home.

One only has to look at the homes we have illustrated in this book to see what magic can be achieved. Fay Gold, Chantal Fabres, Katy Barker, Andrew McIntosh Patrick, Tim Hobby, Alan Siegel, Jackye Lanham, and Stephanie Reeves have all created wonderful homes—and all with totally different tastes in art and photography.

My taste in art is ever changing—partly, I suppose, because I get to see many different artists and mediums in my "day job." There are certain paintings I have always loved and would never want to part with. Others I find I tire of and want to exchange for something new. I often look at the way a painting is framed and realize that a change of frame, and possibly a change of wall or room, will totally rejuvenate my attitude to it. Tastes and styles in framing are changing all the time, and ways of displaying art have also altered quite radically. The rule now seems to be *almost* anything goes. I say "almost" since certain basic rules still exist,

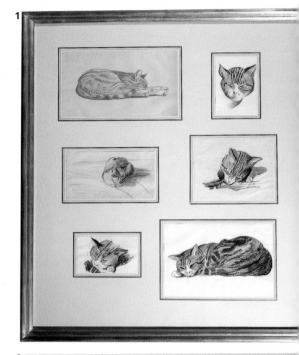

1 A collection of varying sized drawings of cats (circa 1900) framed into one large picture: a way of using different sizes but one subject matter to optimum effect. We often do this in the gallery: any subject will do as long as the drawings are of good quality.

2 Tim Hobby's bedroom has a white headboard that is the perfect spot to hang a photograph. In turn it rests against a many-toned blue-striped wall painted by Hobby himself. A very dramatic, effective display.

and I have tried to make these rules clear in the interviews I have included with experts in all the different fields.

Many new collectors are intimidated about entering a gallery and asking questions. For them the advent of the new art and photography fairs that have sprung up over the past decade are a boon. My advice to them is to go to as many of these art fairs as they can. In large cities like London, New York, and Paris we are spoiled for choice. They range from the Affordable Art Fairs to the very newest and most select fair entitled "Frieze." The best place to find out when and where these fairs take place is a good art or photography magazine, as most of them will list fairs at home and abroad. Try them before you sign up for a subscription because they reflect different styles and interests.

Another useful hint is, whenever you go to a new town, get a copy of a gallery guide. This will be up to date and far better than any list we could hope to give you. In our sources section at the back of the book, however, we include details of galleries we know, which have assisted us in providing the book with good illustrations, as a guide to where to find this sort of art. We have also listed journals worldwide and a few good art show companies as a starting point. We have tried to be as far-reaching as possible, but with framers, for example, you will find that we have only listed the framers with whom we have worked directly ourselves. (I believe that finding a framer should be like finding a hairdresser—get a recommendation from a friend you trust and try them for yourselves but once you find one whose work you like, trust his judgment.)

My children, Michael and Kelly, have played a large part in my appreciation of contemporary trends. This has not meant that I no longer love my collection of early portraits or my religious art from South and Central America, but that I see the beauty of these latest trends, too, and you will find many of them reflected in the pages of this book.

It has been a great experience for me to work with the experts from many different areas of the art world that I have dealt with in this book.

3 I love Amanda Eliasch's multi-image photography: framing very similar images, all 16 of them, in a dramatic frame is an extremely effective way of making a strong impact. The entrance hall of Eliasch's home is hung with her multi-image photography and is quite stunning.

It is always a surprise to find how generous the truly talented are—and how willing they are to share their knowhow and their passion. I believe that together we have compiled a great deal of information into a form in which it can be easily assimilated, both by the aspiring beginner as well as the well-established collector. The information is specialized, varied, informative, and practical.

I am a believer in buying from the soul—buying the art or photography that makes your heart sing, that enlarges your vision, that gives your life new meaning. Others will tell you to buy as an investment. I don't believe this. All of the really great collections I have ever seen have been built on a dream, a love, and a lifetime passion. This is something that will find reflected in the pages that follow, and that, I hope, will inspire you to develop your own collection of art for your home.

Choosing Pictures

What to Collect

I don't really believe in doing things by the book. Rules are meant to be broken. They are only there as guidelines, and as soon as one has developed a sense of style and confidence, it is time to bend—and finally even break—all the hard-and-fast rules that one keeps hearing about.

I believe that many mediums can be hung together to great effect, as in Chantal Fabres' wonderful home (see pages 42–43). Photographs and paintings hang in perfect harmony, giving an eclectic, individual look to her collection. Adding a pinch of imagination and inspiration is far better than sticking resolutely to the same sort of picture. A set of six almost-matching engravings, hung with perfect symmetry, is one way of making sure you are not putting a foot wrong, but it can also be quite dull.

Unless you are very confident, always try a picture out overnight at home prior to buying it. (Most galleries are very happy to allow this.) Some pictures come alive and glow once they reach your home; others immediately look wrong the moment you get them there. Trial and error is a very good way of building an effective collection.

Remember that collectors who buy with their hearts and not their heads are often those whose collections we lust after in later years. If

Previous page: Sarah Morthland has created a gallery effect with fine photography, all silver gelatin prints, framed simply and well, hung over a fine set of nineteenth-century American primitive chairs inherited from her grandparents.

1 The library in Chantal Fabres' home has an unusual bright southern feel to it, helped by the shade of red used. In this room Fabres has chosen one really strong photograph by Luis Gonzalez Palma.

2 The large oil by Radcliffe Bailey on the main wall of Fay Gold's living room dominates this photograph. The '50s furniture, the design of the house (by Stan Topol), and the architecture (by Gold's son) merge together to form one glorious whole.

you try to buy art as an investor, you are unlikely to end up with either paintings you love or a collection of great value. It is buying with "an eye" and a sensibility that does this.

I shall illustrate, in this book, some of the many sorts of art that are available to collect today. The choice is enormous: from antique to modern, figurative to abstract. Photography ranges from the vintage, artistic, or historical to newsworthy pictures taken by young, living photographers. It may be iconic, atmospheric, or portraiture. Tribal and ethnic art have become mainstream, while drawings can still be collected (both old and new). Other collectible media include prints and maps. The choice of subject matter is equally huge: so much depends on what really interests you, what excites you, what works in your home and on your walls.

Try to be eclectic, to be imaginative, to be adventurous. Look carefully at the walls we show you, at what the people we consider to be stylish, informed, and exciting have done. Look at the different combinations of pictures, the choice of images, the juxtaposition, and find something you like. Use it to give you inspiration, assistance, and guidance in building your collection.

1 A fine collection of American portraits has been put together by Stephanie Reeves and hung by Jackye Lanham and Roddie Harris, with the addition of at least one mirror, resulting in a fine dining room wall. Portraits are wonderful hung together —this has been a fashionable collecting theme for centuries and is as strong now as ever.

2 Nina Campbell has hung a lovely pair of '30s watercolors over a Biedermeyer chest

in her apartment. The feel of the apartment is very twentieth century, and the combination of contemporary art and Biedermeyer works extremely well in this drawing room.

3 The work of François Bard is much collected in France and America. His large strong oils of his French bulldog and his Jack Russell friend are much loved. Here we illustrate two limited edition prints by Bard in bold metal frames—strong masculine images perfect for a contemporary space.

Photography

Photography has never been more sought after, more collected than it is today. Throughout the world, the young, hip, and stylish are searching for exciting new talent, for that wonderful, rare vintage print. Many are true collectors, who know their subject and the pitfalls to avoid. Others are beginners, trying to spot talent before it becomes well known.

There are great collections all over the world, and they are all made from different standpoints. It may be a particular subject—such as tiger-hunting in the British Raj or automobile racing—or it may be a particular photographer. The permutations are endless.

Michael Hoppen and Max Caffell's advice will help any collector find their way through the maze of material on the market. Read up on the subject. There are several good guides to collecting photography. Once you have chosen a particular subject, photographer, or period, most good bookshops offer a selection of titles to help pursue the theme. As with all collections, go to exhibitions, attend auctions. The more you learn, the better your collection will be and the more you will enjoy it.

1 "Singing Stone" by Steve Wood, who captured the young Mick Jagger performing in 1976. The perfect example of material that can be found to start a collection of, say, rock legends.

2 A New York skyline by the inimitable Horst Hamann. Hamann's images of the sky and skyscrapers are awe-inspiring and immensely decorative. I prefer them printed in a large format for maximum dynamism.

3 Four square photographs by Marina Berio have been simply but very stylishly framed and hung as a perfect square in the Atlanta loft of Tim Hobby. Perfect symmetry and elegance are achieved by combining superb and dramatic photography with quiet display for maximum effect.

1

1 It is evident that Alan Siegel has collected photography with love and from the heart. Most of the really great collections are built this way, and the Siegel collection is one of them. The curator, Miles Barth, adds a perfect aesthetic, shown in his choice of framing and his perfect sense of space. Here we see "The Pyramid" by Lynn Davis and "Portrait of S. J. Perlman" by Irving Penn.

2 I like Siegel's point that the one thing we all collect is family photography. Not everyone would define this as collecting, but one's family photographs define who we are and where we have come from. The library in Siegel's home is filled with photographs of his family, past and present, and is always being added to and amended.

2

Collecting photographs

Michael Hoppen
Dealer in photographic art and gallery owner

Collecting anything can become an obsession—especially as one begins to understand the finer points of collecting interest. It should, however, also be great fun. Photography has attracted a large following over the past 20 years, partly because of the variety of subject matter and practioners from all over the world. It has recently become one of the most sought after collectibles. Museums, publishers, and institutions have responded to the renewed interest in the medium.

The Victorians collected photography during its early days, when its obvious connections with new technology (during an age when art and science were inextricably entwined) made it a hugely popular pastime. A collector market was born. Photography as a collectible was, however, largely ignored between the wars and up until the early 1970s. Today digitization of the image has created a fresh wave of interest as this new technology becomes widely available to photographers, artists, and, ultimately, the collectors of this brave new format.

Photographs are often relatively easy to find in flea markets and secondhand book stores, as well as the somewhat more adventurous art galleries; but good quality early or "vintage" material has, over the past few years, become harder to find as more collectors have joined the market for nineteenth- and early twentieth-century prints. Traders have also become wise to the sums that have been achieved at auction and have recognized the value of the work they once consigned to folders simply marked "old photos." Fortunately, there are now more and more galleries specializing in photographic works of art, and some cities, such as New York, London, and Paris, have magazines devoted solely to listing exhibitions and galleries that have work for sale. One can move onto more contemporary work, often shown in contemporary art galleries, but it is often the patina and historical resonance of earlier material that attracts collectors initially.

It certainly helps to learn about the different "types" of photographs, of which there are many, and whether the condition of a particular piece will affect its long-term value. Like any collectible, there are criteria that will help one initially. First, is the artist well known and is their work featured in collections and books that reflect consistency of quality and vision? Second, is the photograph well made? (This is harder to determine without a trained eye, but quality often shines through. The older a piece of work, the easier, in a way, it is to see how the "process" has survived the test of time and the vagaries of storage.) And, finally, is the photograph a vintage piece of work? The acceptable definition of "vintage" is a print that was developed within a year of the negative being made. This is hard to check without information on the provenance, and often technical knowhow and equipment (such as a black light) can be useful for dating twentieth-century work. Vintage prints are often much more expensive than "later prints." A simple analogy is the first-edition book market, where a collector is likely to pay substantially more for a signed first edition of a title in preference to a second or third edition of the same book.

Contemporary photography has made substantial inroads into the art-collecting market, including some of the most influential work produced over the past 30

years. This area is also well worth looking at from a collector's point of view and, with notable exceptions, can be a relatively inexpensive way to start a collection. Remember, some of the greatest and most respected artists of the twentieth century were once new and unknown, and were collected by the few who believed in their own judgment.

It is important to buy what you like. Buy with your eye and not with your ears. If a particular photograph rises or falls in value, it is important that regardless of its market value, one still receives great enjoyment from it. Photographs are wonderful objects to hang in your home and mesh well with contemporary living styles, mixing with almost any type of environment. One word of caution that applies to any paper, canvas, or textile: try to place pictures away from radiators, direct sunlight, and varying humidity (which does more harm to most works of art than anything else). A well-made photograph will last for hundreds of years if looked after properly. A badly made "anything" will never last long, regardless of how much one pays.

Suggested reading:

Collecting Photography by Gerry Badger

The Photograph Collectors Guide by Lee D. Witkin and Barbara London

Looking at Photographs by John Szarkowski

A New History of Photography edited by Michel Frizot

1 This elegant dining room is hung with magnificent photography collected by Siegel. The photograph between the sconces is by Kenro.

2 Black-and-white photographs, in different black frames, adorn the red walls of the Firehouse restaurant, a dramatic look that fits well with the period moldings.

3 Alongside a quartet of '50s chairs, a magnificent photograph by Herb Ritts framed in a wide white frame. The striking image of Moscow is by Lane Simmonds.

4 Images of a screen icon are duplicated in a horizontal line and expertly framed in Simon Wilson's home.

5 "Kings of Hollywood" by Slim Aarons. The ultimate iconic photograph: a great glimpse of talent, as well as seductive glamour, at play.

3

4

5

1 Two portraits by Joyce Tenneson from her wonderful book *Light Warriors*, entitled "Jasmin" and "Dasha." They sit well over the great chest in the guest room. I love the ethnographical art. It makes for an eclectic and intelligent look.

2 Photographs taken by Chantal Fabres of her children are placed on a shelf in the bathroom, a charming touch to emulate. Fabres has a good eye not only in buying art and displaying it, but also in her photography.

3 In Katy Barker's light-filled conservatory/dining room, these photographs of sumo wrestlers by Craig McDean add an interesting allure to the space. I am fascinated by the regalia, formality, and tradition of these wrestlers.

The photographic process

Max Caffell
Specialist platinum printer

Photographic prints are produced either on factory-made papers, usually coated with an emulsion of silver gelatin, or by one of the panoply of alternative hand-crafted processes, many of which were pioneered in the 19th century. Many types of silver gelatin paper have been developed over the years. Their stringently controlled finishes create great depth in the image and accurately define the subject matter in beautiful detail.

Most alternative photographic processes require tremendous patience and craftsmanship from the practitioner. With many of these, the artists physically mix the chemistry and hand-coat the papers themselves to produce prints in kaleidoscope metals, inks, or pigments according to the process used and effect required. The enlarger, with its limited tungsten light source, is often replaced by the use of sunlight or specially made ultraviolet light sources. As a result, some processes require a negative to be made the same size as the intended printing paper because they have to be in contact during the exposure of the print – one of the many vagaries of this kind of high-craft image making.

The tonality and surface achievable with these alternative printing processes gives far greater scope and opportunity for expression than can be attained with commercial printing papers. With a hand-crafted platinum print, the result is an image sitting within the paper – as opposed to lying on the surface – creating an extraordinary physical relationship between the viewer and subject. One only has to see the same picture printed in a variety of media to realize how profound an effect differing processes make on the viewer's reaction to an image.

As well as sound aesthetic reasons for using alternative processes, there are also the considerable advantages of printing in some very stable materials. The platinum process, photogravure, and some of the pigment-printing techniques yield very stable and permanent prints – much more so than their silver gelatin counterparts. So, when collecting photographs, it is advantageous to have some insights into how the print has been made as well as how the image appeals to one's emotive sensibilities.

1 Ann Patrick's painting totally dominates the dining room of her brother's home (Andrew McIntosh Patrick). This wonderful painting chronicles a lunch at which they were both guests of a friend in Asolo, Italy, and the painting exudes an atmosphere of summer, friends, good food, and sunshine.

2 In Nina Campbell's drawing room the painting of oversized tulips is by contemporary artist Sophie Coryndon. They are perfect in this light, high-ceilinged room and complement the simple elegant mantle over which they have been hung.

Suggested reading:

British Artists at Work by Amanda Eliasch

Still Life by Norbert Schneider

David Remfry: Dancers

Art

The art on your walls probably says more about you than anything else in your home. We seem to express ourselves most truly by what we choose to hang—or often *not* to hang—on our walls. (Many homes have virtually nothing on their walls; something I find hard to understand.)

Buying art is not like buying a piece of furniture. It has no function other than to bring joy into one's heart and to add an element of pure beauty to the home you are creating. For this reason it needs to be a less logical and functional acquisition. Knowledge and experience are, of course, needed, but there has to be an element of "love at first sight"—and then hopefully at second and third sight, too.

In any large town today there will be at least one good art museum, several galleries, and most importantly, access to an art fair. These are gathering momentum worldwide, and are becoming the most popular way to acquire one's first few purchases. Buying at an art fair has many advantages. You get to see a vast selection of art in different price categories. For those nervous about approaching a gallery, it is neutral territory. You can stay as long as you like without feeling silly, and come back day after day until you are sure. I recommend fairs to any new collector.

A subscription to a good art magazine is also an essential. Not only will it give you details of fairs, but it will include informative articles, advertisements for galleries, and different opinions.

In collecting art, it is the development of the "eye" that counts: for this frequent visits to galleries are the answer. Rent an audio guide for the exhibitions you see, and listen and learn. The more you look, the more you will enjoy—and the more professional your eye will become.

Collecting art

Andrew McIntosh Patrick
of The Fine Art Society, London

Having been an art dealer for nearly 50 years, and for the same time a hyperactive acquirer of "things," I still find it difficult to offer useful advice on collecting.

Not all of the "things" I have collected—Scottish pictures, Japanese prints, nineteenth-century furniture, Christopher Dresser metalwork—have consistently lived in my life. Some have just lived on because they were useful, functional, or needed; however, the majority still satisfy me—even excite me—if only for my being their "owner." While this does not offer much of a directive for collecting, neverthess it allows me, from experience, to suggest some lines of approach.

First, base your "style" on something positive that you feel strongly about; for example, strong color, minimal color (white or non-color), or an ethnic, chic, aspirational, or imitative theme. Having adopted a style find, if you don't feel self-confident, a decorator who understands what (you think) you want. Keep your eyes open for furniture, objects, or decorations that will comfortably coexist with the style you have chosen. Finally, eschew gimmicks; they date and go out of fashion rapidly.

Choosing "art" is the most difficult subject on which to offer advice. However, finding things that coexist with your chosen style will bring a harmony and background to your collection. (Finding an art dealer who is on your wavelength can certainly help).

1

1 In Andrew McIntosh Patrick's library the amazing and unusual furniture that adds to the feeling of a collection built up over time, is by Gerald Summers, makers of furniture from the 1930s.

2 Katy Barker mixes paintings, photographs, and African objects in an eclectic and fascinating way. Her love of all things African is obvious throughout her home.

3 In Fay Gold's large, spacious entrance hall, many paintings and photographs hang together creating a wonderful picture gallery effect.

1 A painting of oversized flowers by Sarah Bredenkamp hangs in the artist's London home over a long dresser. The vibrancy and color of the painting is redolent of her African roots.

2 In the family room of Fay Gold's elegant home, a large painting by Zoe Hersey is hung over a minimal mantel. Gold not only selects magnificent art, but also gauges exactly the correct hanging position and what to hang with what. This room with its '50s furniture, cool atmosphere, and superb sculpture by Dan Corbin is as close to perfection as one can be.

Contemporary art

Dr. S. Maureen Burke

Dean of Academic Initiatives, Savannah College of Art and Design, Georgia

Contemporary art is the art of the new, the now, the present. Strictly defined, it is art that has been created within the last 10 to 15 years. Unlike "modern art," which comprises the art of the entire last century, contemporary art is still evolving.

The media and techniques contemporary artists use are often experimental, such as mixed media, video, or digital media, but these artists also may work in such traditional media as painting, sculpture, and photography. These artworks, created in the present and of the present, reflect a multiplicity of styles. No critical consensus has yet been formed, no established movement has so far come to the forefront. The works stand on their own. They may be serious or humorous, narrative or evocative, figurative or abstract. General themes may include identity, politics, gender, or the representation of the human body. Contemporary artists working in the abstract tradition explore artistic space and the placement of forms in that space. Artists who work with digital media may deal with aspects of time, movement, and change.

Contemporary art is too new to be predictable. There is a sense of discovery as collectors or curators select particular pieces from the vast amount of contemporary work being created. Without the intervention of historical or critical judgment, the role of individual choice becomes paramount. The collector selects work to which they react strongly. This selection is an aesthetic choice, based on the likes or dislikes of an individual.

Viewers enjoy a more direct engagement with contemporary art than with art of earlier periods since the distancing that comes with the passage of time has not yet taken place. Artists working today share the viewers' world, their same time and space. Contemporary art crosses boundaries into the viewers' own experiences and perspectives, enabling them to interact with the work in a very instinctive way. This immediate and intimate visual dialogue, with its sense that critics, collectors, viewers, and artists are together participating in a formative art world, is one of the most profound rewards of contemporary art.

1

2

1 In a corner of Katy Barker's large and light-filled living room, Barker has mixed photography with paintings and objects yet again to create another interesting grouping in the room.

2 In Tim Hobby's apartment, the living room is dominated by a magnificent photograph over the settee by John Folsom entitled "Low Country." It is a silver gelatin print and it adds a most wonderful serenity to the room. On the other wall the top painting is acrylic on canvas by David Shapiro, entitled "Origin and Return 8" (2001).

3 Another aspect of the same room in Hobby's apartment shows a tall vertical painting that looks magnificent on a tall narrow wall and complements the use of horizontal stripes on the other side of the room. This room has been carefully balanced, but nothing is forced or too contrived looking. This is a really important point in collecting and hanging—sometimes people try too hard.

3

Drawings

I have always loved drawings, particularly the drawings of the seventeenth, eighteenth, and nineteenth centuries. There is a refined quality about fine drawings that one really finds in no other aspect of art, in my view. There is also a very quiet beauty and a fascination that can never be ignored.

Although fine drawings have always been much desired, it is still possible, I find, to buy finely executed anonymous drawings—particularly from the nineteenth and early twentieth centuries—that are very beautiful and when well framed and hung can make a truly wonderful wall. I find that people tend to go up really close when they see a drawing or collection of drawings—they seem to inspire inspection!

Framing is particularly important with drawings—old frames are wonderful if you can find them. If not, try to find a framer who can create a sympathetic frame so as to enhance and not overwhelm your drawing. When putting together a collection of drawings, I suggest that you do not necessarily try to pair or team them up, but instead try to make an eclectic mosaic wall. Alternatively, if you find a collection of very small drawings, they can look wonderful mounted together and framed in one big frame. A collection of drawings, when well chosen and hung with panache, can be very dramatic. It is a refined taste, but this does not mean that drawings are dull—far from it, as the picture opposite illustrates.

1 David Remfry's drawings combine the quality of eras long passed with today's subject matter, screaming craft in a world where learning how to draw has seemed out of fashion for some time. Stella McCartney chose him for her first advertising campaign, and it is a credit to her that she did: compulsive viewing.

2 Katy Barker's library is dominated by a perfectly hung collection of drawings together with superb tribal items. A red Tonio Trzebinski and two abstracts by the same artist hang together with a drawing by Giacometti, photography by Roger Ballan, and three magnificent Samburo spears.

Collecting old drawings

Charles Plante
Dealer in fine drawings and watercolors

Drawings are an underrated area of collecting. Unlike painting or sculpture, or the decorative and applied arts, drawings have not been considered prestige objects, and therefore belong to the more subtle world of connoisseurship. Yet draftsmanship was central to art education from the Renaissance until the Impressionist revolution replaced the skill of a precise line with that of color and the brush.

Studies from this great tradition, drawing on the antique sculpture, can be seen in watercolor drawings by Napoleon's architects Percier and Fontaine. Another popular technique is sanguine and black chalk, as in the life-study of a standing male nude. Topographical drawings of subjects such as architecture and gardens are fascinating, as with Samuel Grimm's (1733–1794) late eighteenth-century view of the interior of Holywell Church in North Wales. Landscapes painted in gouache (a technique of combining watercolor with opaque pigments or

"bodycolor") are very desirable for their beauty and use of faint hues, such as the garden outside Toulon, France, by Zacharie-Felix Doumet (1761–1818).

Technical drawings of objects had to be accurate and show precisely a three-dimensional object on paper. Superb examples of technical drawings may be found, such as designers' drawings of clocks and similar pieces, created for craftsmen to execute.

A finely detailed drawing of a late nineteenth-century German drummer by Edward Detaille (1848–1912) combines subtle techniques of line drawing in pencil and ink, with lightly applied watercolor, to create a sparkling effect.

In my collection, I have mixed various drawings and techniques, and enhanced them by using "period" frames. My inspiration is the private cabinets and princely collections of drawings from the Renaissance onward, the more personal Grand Tour collections, especially for the British aristocracy, which in the nineteenth and twentieth centuries inspired the prints and drawings rooms of the great public collections, from the Louvre in Paris to the Metropolitan Museum.

Where are the sources to buy from today? Clearly the big names attract rival collectors or museums; for example, a recently reattributed Michelangelo "Study for a Mourning Woman" from Castle Howard was purchased at auction for £5.94 million ($8.4 million) at Sotheby's. However, there are still chances to buy "attributed to," "circle of," "school of," or "style of" examples. An unattributed drawing may lack an artist's name, but that does not make it any less interesting, and with advancing scholarship a name might one day be attached to it.

There is a greater chance to make a 'find' when building a collection of drawings, as the margin for error is greater in a field with, sometimes, hundreds of examples of a single artist's work. Dealers and auction houses are still the best source for finding drawings with researched attributions. For the lesser or unknown masters, there is still the chance for a discovery. Folios, sketchbooks, and individual sheets asking to be reattributed still appear, with the opportunity to discover a "sleeper" or unidentified sheet lurking with even some of the biggest auction houses or dealers.

1 "Study of Rabbits" by Maria Teresa Faini, a Florentine artist working today in the old style. Sanguine, the color of blood, is drawn with red chalk and was a great favorite in the 1700s.

2 The interior of Holywell Church, North Wales. A late-eighteenth-century drawing by Samuel Grimm.

3 "The Great Circle" is by Christopher Hill. Katy Barker has surrounded it with candlesticks and ancient objects to maximum effect. Each object has been chosen to add dimension to this fascinating picture.

3

1 W. Graham Arader III has hung the separately published sections from this wall map depicting North America by Henry Popple, 1733, over the stairwell of his New York home. This is the first wall map of the American colonies and a fascinating collectors' item.

2 In a corner of her apartment, filled throughout with fine prints and watercolors, Janis Aldridge has this eighteenth-century hand-colored engraving of a botanical illustration framed imaginatively in a mixture of gold and silver finishes.

Suggested reading:

The Mapping of America by Seymour Schwartz

The Mapping of the World by Rodney Shirley

2

Other Media

Today, a large choice of alternative items is available to hang on one's walls. One may choose tribal and ethnic art, for example. As the taste for exotic holidays has increased, so has the popularity of Navaho blankets, African masks, Indian carvings, and Polynesian objects (to name but a few). Tapestries are a somewhat acquired taste, but textiles of different kinds are now very popular. Modern weavings, antique quilts, ethnic fabrics, and indeed fashion as art are all possibilities. Early decorative maps have long been a serious collecting field, as have movie posters.

Single mirrors, as well as collections of mirrors, appear more and more often on the walls of the ultra chic. They are an effective medium. I have always had a penchant for not only adding a mirror or two to a wall, but also pieces of carving. These give an exciting finish to a display.

On collecting

W. Graham Arader III
Antique map and print dealer

There are two factors shared by the greatest and most successful of collectors: the passionate desire to possess, and the rational ability to learn.

There are myriad ways that collectors can protect themselves from making mistakes. They can go to museums and libraries to see exhibitions and established collections; they can talk to and visit other collectors, dealers, and curators; they can buy reference books, and attend auctions and fairs before ever spending any money. Visiting experienced collectors in their homes is probably the fastest way to gain the knowledge to build an elegant collection of one's own in a relatively short period of time.

Perhaps it is a wise idea to wait six months to two years before spending any money. As their experience and expertise grows, most collectors end up regretting—and even selling—their early purchases. The longer one waits, the fewer mistakes are made. At the same time, this describes a collector who lacks the passionate need to own. In my experience, collectors who have such self control (read: lack of true passion) that they can deny their collecting impulses for two years, risk building collections that lack style, panache, and flair. The most exciting purchases, and those that lead to the most enduring satisfaction and the best collections, are driven by pure, uncontrollable desire, in tandem with some degree of expert advice.

With regard to investment, the best rewards inevitably come to those who throw caution to the wind and are willing to pay—even to overpay—for the highest level of quality. Those instead with a plodding, cerebral plan to reap financial rewards never—in my experience—have done so.

Charles Montgomery, my instructor on eighteenth-century American furniture, puts it best: "Whereas in the joy of a treasure one forgets a high price paid, in the possession of the second-rate one remembers only its cheapness." This has been my guiding principle for 35 years!

1 Sarah Morthland has gathered together a fascinating group of very different objects and folk art that contrasts well with the fine photography in this lovely apartment. The long, narrow painting of apples is by Stephen Bear.

2 Penny Drue Baird has hung Debuffet prints floor to ceiling in an imaginative and striking way across the entire wall of a narrow hall. This requires great attention or it can look messy.

3 In Carolyn MacKenzie's New York apartment the ox-blood walls are a perfect foil for the eighteenth-century French hand-painted panels that fit within the moldings. This is an inspired look for a dining room.

Collecting prints

Sarah Soames
Former head of Christies' Natural History Books

Although printmaking has always been an art form in its own right, it must not be forgotten that, before the invention of photography, it was the only means available of producing repeatable visual images on paper. It is hard to imagine the world before modern communications, before transportation as we know it, before the internet – and before photography, a world where prints were the only way of distributing pictures and maps. Imagine the first engraved views of Australia; the illustrations in the accounts of Captain Cook's voyages; the first pictures of the New World; the Daniells' views of India; portraits, costumes, and customs of illustrious foreign lands; images of the flora and fauna of faraway countries. Imagine the impact of these images.

Also, printing was employed for utilitarian as much as for aesthetic ends, and from the very earliest days of the printing press, books on all subjects were produced with engraved illustrations. These, of course, included illustrations by prominent artists of the time. So it can truly be said that there are prints illustrating every subject known to man, painstakingly hand-produced for the enlightenment of our forefathers. It is a list far too long to contemplate here, so I can only scratch the tip of the iceberg, mention a few household names, and hope to convey some of the magic and romance of print collecting. Prints can be discovered in many places: flea markets, antique fairs,

1 In Jackye Lanham's dining room a pair of pictures are placed one on top of another between a pair of antique gilded sconces. Pairs hanging in this way, rather than side by side, have more punch. The pictures are a great touch as they add texture and great interest to the room. The carved walnut baskets of wheat and fruit have been gilded and make a most unusual pair.

2 and 3 The interior design of the wonderful kitchen that Jackye Lanham created for an Atlanta client is truly great, with all the Lanham touches of comfort and style. Lanham has used in one case a collection of clocks to decorate a wall and in another a marvelous collection of pewter chargers. I think that large kitchens cry out for imaginative picture hanging, and I love the use of objects rather than pictures here. The platters over the metal hood are magnificent.

auction rooms, print shops, and so on, within reach of all pockets and to suit all tastes. But be careful with Old Master prints; this is an area that can be something of a minefield without a certain amount of knowledge and expertise.

The variety of painting techniques that developed over the centuries to produce these illustrations, creating images with different qualities and effects, is an interesting and complicated technical subject. Bamber Gascoigne has bravely tackled it in his much-needed guide *How to Identify Prints, A Complete Guide to Manual and Mechanical Processes from Woodcut to Inkjet*, published in 1986. The Henry Cole Wing at the Victoria and Albert Museum in London is well worth a visit. It includes a section devoted to printing techniques, with printmakers' tools and examples of their crafts displayed and explained. These include the earliest woodcuts, copperplate etching and engraving, mezzotint, aquatint, lithography, steel engraving, and so on to the present day. Since the advent of photography, and the availability of alternative methods of reproduction, printmaking has continued to develop as an independent art form, and we are all familiar with the look of many of today's prints.

In fact, today, at the mention of prints, most people think of a screen print, say an Andy Warhol or Roy Lichtenstein, or one of any number of limited editions by contemporary artists. Like everything else, decorative prints are subject to the whims of fashion, and today's interiors call for colorful abstract images, the more way-out the better.

4 Stephanie Reeves of Atlanta utilizes an oval mirror in her large kitchen/dining room, and has cleverly hung a fabulous collection of gelatin molds all around it. Not easy to collect or hang, but worth it for the stunning visual effect.

5 Stephanie Reeves has hung two rows of three nineteenth-century gentlemen in her husband's dressing room, and this formal array gives perfect balance and style.

6 Roddie Harris, the maestro picture hanger, has used an amusing collection of skittles as alternative wall decoration. It has humor and is most effective.

Choosing Subject

People

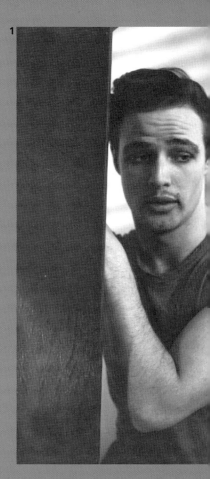

1

We all love pictures of people. This has always been the case, and it would seem to me that it will always be so. The obsession with celebrity photographs in our news-papers and magazines is, I am sure, only a recent and up-to-date manifestation of the popularity of the portraits of such people as Holbein. After all, it is through his art that we visualize life in Tudor Britain and the love life of the king!

Many of the greatest and most loved artists have been best known for their portraits and their exquisite and painstaking reproduction of the clothing and jewelry of times past. Such images are held in both our consciousness and subconsciousness, and stay with us forever. Everyone has his or her favorite image.

With photography it is even more the case that the images we remember are of people: images of people—known and unknown—that define a moment and an era, an expression and a style, a beauty. It could be a kiss on a street in Paris, two strangers embracing in joy at the end of the war, Jackie Kennedy and her children standing with such sorrow and dignity at the funeral of President Kennedy, or the face of Marilyn Monroe.

1 "Marlon Brando" by Ronny Jacques. This brooding young Brando was, and still is, an icon of raw sexuality and opened up a world of new and tougher heroes than the suave Gable, Peck, and Grant.

2 "James Joyce" by Georges Sheridan, who lives in the hill village of Deia in Mallorca. His paintings are filled with light and color.

3 "Bibi et Denise Grey à bord du Dahu II, juillet 1926" by Jacques Henri Lartigue (1894–1986), from a posthumous limited-edition collection of platinum prints issued by the Ministère de la Culture, France/AAJHL. The elegance, sensitivity, and quality of Lartigue's photography are incomparable.

1 Jackie Onassis leaving Claridges hotel, by Ted West. Jackie Kennedy Onassis was the ultimate style icon for almost half a century, for much of that time her every appearance created paparazzi frenzy and acres of newsprint. She was American royalty.

2 The Harley Davidson, now 100 years old, is the ultimate icon to a host of middle-aged men, who include riders from all walks of life. Doctors, lawyers, and accountants travel alongside more 'traditional' bikers.

1

Icons

There are certain photographs that are iconic. Either they so encapsulate all one's emotions and memories of a particular person or movie or event in one's life, or they capture a single moment in their story, when the entire world stopped breathing for a second and forevermore remembered where they were at that point in time. Everyone remembers where they were when Kennedy was shot, and the photographs tend to bring that moment back to life.

It's not only tragedies that bring forth iconic photographs. Stills from movies have the same effect in happier ways—a finely honed image can trigger a sensation or feeling; a memory. A moment of rare clarity never to be totally forgotten. It has been hard to choose these few pictures from the multitude of images available. I decided that only photographs really illustrate what I am saying about icons—somehow the immediacy of film is the only medium that can create a truly iconic picture.

2

What makes an icon

Lucy Yeoman
Editor, Harpers & Queen *Magazine*

What is it that makes someone an icon? Which qualities must a person possess, or at least be attributed with, to turn them from just another celebrity into someone whose star shines as brightly—if not more so—long after they are gone. The world's greatest icons define a particular era or a specific chapter in world history; they are the distillation of all that was held true at that time. Often they bring to mind a certain mood or emotion and, particularly where females are concerned, redefine ideals of beauty, style, or sexuality. Think of Jacqueline Kennedy, a woman whose mere image invokes one of the most important moments in American history, whose petite frame and huge black sunglasses alone summon up the grief of an entire nation, whose unique style has influenced generations of women in her wake.

The most powerful of icons are often associated with a particular image, be it an unforgettable paparazzi shot, a controversial portrait, or just a few seconds of compelling television footage. The role of iconographer thus assumes a great importance.

3

3 Greta Garbo as Mata Hari the international spy, by Clarence Sinclair Bull. The inscrutable haunting beauty of Garbo and her need 'to be alone' made her recognizable worldwide, and the catchphrase has lived on.

4 Steve McQueen has probably outstripped even Brando as the rough, tough, taciturn screen hero and icon to men and women alike. It is hard to describe his incredible attraction, but one only has to flick through the William Claxton book of photographs of Steve McQueen to see that these are images that will live forever.

4

1 Audrey Hepburn as Holly Golightly in *Breakfast at Tiffany's*—so iconic that I can hear the strains of "Moon River" as I look at it! Will there ever be a perfect face and figure like this again? Audrey Hepburn made us care about every character she portrayed.

2 Pablo Picasso by Arnold Newman. Everything about Picasso is here. His strength of character, awe-inspiring talent, obstinacy and his immense masculinity.

On photography

William Conran
Celebrity photographer

The decisive moment in photography often occurs immediately after the photographer has pressed the shutter release. In order for the picture to have impact, the image will have been anticipated fractions of a second before the moment has arrived. In a burst of, say, four exposures, there will only be one image that captures the mood, timing, and atmosphere that the photographer has in mind. The process is often purely instinctive and is always a surprise. Invariably the final image will never need a caption or explanation. Nowadays, with the increasing use of digital cameras, the pressure is on photographers to send images quickly to their respective agencies or publications, so there is less time to have a considered viewpoint. In this way a truly decisive moment may be missed due to time restraints.

In the past, the great photographers, such as Bert Hardy and Henri Cartier-Bresson, were using equipment so basic and mechanical that their craft came through in all its true simplicity. In the modern age of digital photography, we're thinking more about technology than photography as art. Perhaps we have lost something in the process; the time in the darkroom, considered framing, and just sheer instinct. However, no matter what we use to capture images, there will always be decisive moments. Let us hope that we will always be able to recognize them when we see them.

1

3 Frida Kahlo caught in a thoughtful pose by an unknown photographer, wearing one of her many Mexican folk costumes. Kahlo has slowly and steadily become one of the most significant, and fascinating female artists and icons in the world today.

4 Marilyn Monroe emerging from a limo at a Hollywood premiere by Murray Garrett. Not a week goes by when I don't come across yet another vulnerable or immensely glamorous photograph of Marilyn. It seems bizarre that the ultimate icon was so lacking in self-confidence.

2

3

4

Suggested reading:

Steve McQueen by William Claxton

Allure by Diana Vreeland

Marilyn Monroe by Eve Arnold

Evidence: 1944–1994 by Richard Avedon

Once There Was a Way: Photographs of the Beatles by Harry Benson

Judy Garland: A Portrait in Art and Anecdote by John Fricke and Lorna Luft

1 Collin Wiggin's and Frank Auerbach's portrait from the series "Double Vision" (1997). A fine contemporary portrait in total contrast to those of earlier centuries. The traditional portrait is alive and well, but one now has the choice of many other genres showing life as lived today.

2 One of a pair of "his and hers" portraits from the nineteenth century, interesting in that not only do we have the lady of the household and her children formally dressed in their Sunday best, but also the trappings of wealth are there painted as carefully as the features of the sitters.

3 "Portrait of a Maharajah," painted circa 1890 by E. A. Harris in a Gainsborough-like style to show that the sitter was as grand as the English lords. I love the costume and fabulous jewelry as well as the silks of the clothing.

4 "Portrait of a Young Man," oil on canvas, by Jacob Ferdinand Voet. The ultimate seventeenth-century portrait of a European gentleman: an accomplished artist, a good-looking sitter, and magnificent clothing. For those of us who love faces, these paintings are very desirable.

5 Richard Philp has provided us with this perfect portrait of a child and dog. Somehow the clothing of the children in these early portraits is even more overwhelming in detail and quality than that of their parents.

Portraits

Portraits never date—they are somehow always current, always exciting, and always desirable. I have more portraits in my home than any other genre of painting, drawing, or photograph. I have a complete wall of religious paintings from Central America, South America, Russia, and Greece; portraits of Venetian princes and princesses by Bosquet on another wall, and many more conventional portraits on walls all over the apartment.

I began to wonder why I find myself drawn to costume and faces—the aspects of portraits that fascinate many collectors. I suspect that what one chooses to hang on one's walls has a lot to do with one's own personality—I am drawn to people more than objects and theories.

Although sitters tend, I am sure, to prepare their faces and poses for the painter or photographer, I suspect that often a very real and unstudied persona is captured by the artist. This gives portraits, for me, their vulnerability; their reality; their fascination.

Suggested reading:

Faces: A Narrative History of the Portrait in Photography by Ben Maddow

Julia Margaret Cameron by Helmut Gernsheim

August Sander: People of the 20th Century edited by Susanne Lange-Greve

Diane Arbus: An Aperture Monograph

In the American West by Richard Avedon

1 This totally contemporary, yet completely figurative, portrait of a young woman exemplifies the perfect modern portrait. Jennifer Anderson has achieved the all-round satisfaction that a truly fine portrait possesses without the stiffness of a more conventional work.

2 A striking, almost Velasquez-like painting by Armando Seijo depicts another type of modern portrait: a contemporary woman is pictured in a much earlier style but with a totally modern attitude. This juxtaposition works extremely well.

3 A portrait of the dancer Trisha Brown from Joyce Tenneson's great book *Wise Women*. Tenneson celebrates the insights, courage, and beauty of women aged from 65 to 100, and her sepia-toned portraits are fascinating and electrifying.

4 "Hats" by Milt Kobayashi (oil on canvas) depicts a woman sitting pensively amid a collection of hats. I like this sort of contemporary portrait in which the surroundings are as important as the person portrayed.

1

Elizabethan portraiture

Richard Philp
World expert on Elizabethan portraits

It was 1965, I had just opened my gallery and was awaiting my first customer. He duly arrived, introducing himself as Joseph Murumbi, vice president of Kenya, head of the Masai tribe and collector of Western art. Joe wasted no time in purchasing my "first" Elizabethan portrait: a study on panel of a young girl of the 1590s, and so began a collection of ashen lead white-faced portraits to be displayed in a Moorish residence in Africa.

In the 1960s I realized that the school of English painting from 1158 to 1603 had been entirely neglected. But Elizabethan portraiture, far from being the poor cousin of European Renaissance art, was magnificent. The Reformation in northern Europe had put an end to Catholic subject matter: secular portraiture practiced by fleeing Huguenot painters became the popular—and virtually the only—subject matter. The Queen herself instigated the stress on 'linear' at the expense of 'chiaroscuro' (light and shade).

Portraits of Elizabeth I are rare, but they occasionally turn up. Visiting a provincial art gallery I noticed an odd-looking three-quarter-length portrait of a 1920s flapper girl, the paint peeling away, revealing fragments of what appeared to be sixteenth-century pigment. I bought it and cleaned off the entire '20s surface to discover a magnificent coronation portrait of Elizabeth painted by the finest portraitist of the day—Hans Eworth.

Italian fifteenth-century works have also always fascinated me. Some years ago I discovered in a saleroom cardboard box a nineteenth-century painted panel of "St. John The Baptist." I noticed a fragment of early pigment beneath the surface. I bought it, cleaned it, and revealed a previously unknown masterpiece of a young woman's profile by the Renaissance master Fra Bartolomeo—friend to Leonardo and teacher to Raphael. The discovery helped confirm my motives for studying portraiture: it encompasses all sensitive human values—compassion, the spiritual, the romantic, and the aesthetic.

Whether it is a late Rembrandt self-portrait, a Goya study, or a simple oil sketch by Fra Bartolomeo, portraiture remains the supreme subject among all.

1 "Fourteen Studies of Blue," charcoal, by Jenny Thompson. Thompson explains the title came about as Blue is the name of a girl, and the 14 studies are of her dancing. In this charcoal study, the line drawings give strength and expression to the sentiments of the subjects.

2 "Funny Feet" by Karin Rosenthal (1989). A fascinating combination of both beautiful bodies and quirky humor. This would contrast well in a collection of beautiful bodies if shown with a classical nude, a partial body, or even a photograph of a classical statue.

3 "Lips" by Henry Horenstein. A black-and-white fiber print toned sepia. This is from Horenstein's book *Humans*. His work is both compelling and magical. He seems to make the mundane very special. I like to juxtapose a part of something with the whole.

4 "Jenny Torso" by Allan Jenkins. Jenkins says, "I am fascinated by the way light makes people and objects look magical and ethereal," and indeed his work does have that brooding dreamy quality, giving this beautiful body a totally different spirit to any of the others selected.

Body Beautiful

The most interesting aspect of the body beautiful is, without doubt, the extraordinary change that has taken place over the ages in the desirable and acceptable shape, size, and style of both the female and male body. The romantic concept of womanhood in the sixteenth century—and for the centuries that followed—was a voluptuous one with wonderful fleshy tones and mellow colors. Even the dressed women showed wondrous expanses of female sexuality with their low-cut dresses and corseted waists. World War I seems to have changed forever both women's views of themselves and the artists' (male) view of women, at least in the West. As women took over the jobs of the men who were fighting and dying, their dress, behavior, and shape seemed to change, never to return to the rampant, fleshy sexuality of the past.

In the Renaissance the ideal man must have been Michelangelo's David. Today, somehow both men and women have as an ideal the same, almost androgynous, body and style of dress. Women and men often wear almost the same clothing. Slimness and fitness are supremely desirable—breasts are small and hips nonexistent—at least in the ideal.

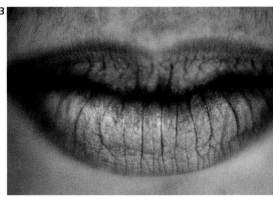

Suggested reading:

The Body: Photographs of the Human Form by William Ewing

A Perspective of Nudes by Bill Brandt

Storyville Portraits by E. J. Bellocq

4

1 "Nude in Yellow Chair" by Georges Sheridan. Sheridan's nudes have a sleepy sensuality that one relates to sunny climes. His women are very real. I have found that adding a painting by Sheridan to a home adds light and warmth in an extraordinary sensuous way.

2 Number 10 from a series entitled "Bordello" by Vee Speers, fresson charcoal print. This print of the ladies of the bordello looking at themselves in a mirror has a wonderful *fin de siècle* feel: a sort of latter-day Toulouse-Lautrec. Speers has captured a very Parisian feel.

3 "Nude Beneath the Moon" in an octagonal glass "agate" frame by Suzy Bartolini. Bartolini is a well-known French artist who uses the technique *églamisée*—or reverse painting on glass. The glowing jewel-like effect Bartolini obtains this way is extraordinary.

4 "Nu Horizontal" by Lorioz. The paintings of Lorioz have captured the hearts of art buyers on both sides of the Atlantic. Her ladies are large, but they are beautifully large and voluptuous, and whenever we place one in our window, everyone stops, looks, smiles, and is tempted.

3
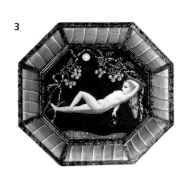

1

2

4

The human figure

Sandra J. Reed

Dean of Graduate Studies, The Savannah College of Art and Design, Georgia

Today the human figure is as pertinent and powerful a subject of art as it was to the ancient Greeks, after whose work so much is modeled. Figure drawing, usually executed in charcoal, serves as the basis for any fine artist's education. For many artists, drawing or painting from life becomes a mainstay of their repertoire, offering myriad possibilities for reflection and design by using different lighting, poses, settings or drapery. The awareness acquired through this study informs work in other media and inspires many artists to rely upon their training to create figurative works constructed from their imagination and memory.

The portrayal of the female nude is inseparable from a conception of fine art. Studies in the history of art, psychology, theology, sociology, perception, philosophy, and mathematics have taken the image of the female nude as a subject, and offer profound insights for understanding the persistence of the subject. The phenomenum of nudity as a state distinct from nakedness (as illustrated by Adam and Eve) has been developed and interpreted variously by theorists. Whether the subject is the passive object of the viewer's study or returns the viewer's gaze is also a key interpretive factor and continues to be explored relative to a feminist perspective.

The relationship between the amount of surface area occupied by the figure and that which is not the figure is of central importance, giving the perimeter of the work significance whether the portrayed figure is cropped ("touching" the edge) or not. The foreground, the bottom few inches of the work, is psychologically empowered, establishing relative proximity by either setting the figure back in pictorial space or placing the figure within reach. In a great work of art, the proportions of the portrayed figure are balanced in their importance by the function of negative space, or the shapes and intervals between forms, together establishing the meaning of the work.

Whether idealized goddess or imperfect individual, female subjects are empowered as the artist's impression of both his or her own humanity and the universal human condition.

Observing Life

Photography seems to be the ideal medium to capture moments—
moments of life—often termed vernacular photography. These pictures
can truly say more than a thousand words, and I have tried to select
images here that say so very much in a captured instant. The work of
Robert Doisneau has particular relevance, and I have listed the illustrated catalog of his work below for those who want to see more of these
fascinating glimpses of Paris life. The great Lartigue was a past master at
showing the truly elegant moments he glimpsed on the Côte d'Azur—no
one could better evoke that entire glamorous time.

1 This image, entitled "Jim Eicke, Bell Ranch" is from a collection of photographs by Martin H. Schreiber. The book is called *Last of a Breed, Portraits of Working Cowboys*—and is just that. They are not Hollywood counterparts but real life contemporary cowboys.

2 This image of a late '60s London coffee bar by Alex Dellow has to be a trip down memory lane for anyone who was around in London at the time. What a perfect start for a sixties collection. It could include photographers, models, Carnaby Street, hot pants, and coffeepots!

3 "Priscilla" from a series called "Almost Grown" by Joseph Szabo. This young girl casually smoking is truly an image of "Observing Life." It is a side of life we do not like and yet it is fascinating. It is an extremely sought after image by Szabo, and it haunts me.

4 A policeman in Washington, DC, by Weegee. He produced a book in 1945 called *Weegee's Naked City* that was made into a film. As a news photographer and chronicler of New York city from the 1930s to the 1950s, his work has proved unforgettable.

5 An image from "Paris Life" by Robert Doisneau entitled "La Vitrine Galerie Romi, 6ème Arrondissement, Paris 1949: Le Regard Oblique." It could only be a scene from a Paris street. Scenes of Paris make a wonderful collection.

We have also selected paintings illustrating moments—but they are of a totally different type. They have to be much more contrived by definition because they take so much longer to achieve.

The relevance of all these images, be they vernacular photography or more contrived paintings, is that their popularity and desirability are as much because of the memories or sentiments they provoke—different in each viewer—as in the beauty of the actual work. The sensation of a time passed by; the memory of a relationship long gone; the taste and smell of a city or street remembered in a flash. Looking at one's own photograph albums, the sensation can often be the same. Strangely, it is not always the expected image that has the most effect.

4

5

Our common bond

Miles Barth
Author, editor and independent curator

One of life's experiences that most of us share is the practice of collecting photographs. Whether they are of our parents or grandparents, images made at birthdays or picnics, these photographic pictures somehow accumulate in our drawers and boxes. As it is said of language that's the everyday speech of a people or group, these everyday images can also be called "vernacular."

Beginning in the late 1880s, when George Eastman introduced the Brownie (named for a legendary elf that performed good deeds at night), photography became accessible to the average person. The term "snapshot" was coined shortly after the enormous success of the roll-film camera at about this same time, making photography a ubiquitous and easy-to-use accessory of modern life.

Over the decades, cameras began appearing at almost every kind of social event—any occasion that warranted visual documentation. These photographs reflected the spirit of their time in refreshingly honest and often unexpected ways. Even today, with the advent of digital photography, we tend to take the same kind of images. Vernacular photography is all around us, the work of anonymous amateurs whose happy accidents and successful failures result in images that we save and cherish. We are surrounded by these images, on our desks, refrigerators, coffee tables, and dressers. They remind us of our loved ones, both living and dead, friends from school, distant relatives. Photographs help us keep track of our children as they grow. They record the profound and silly rituals of our children's lives, from graduations to ball games, from vacations to the births of their own offspring.

Just as collectors of rare photographs protect their images as art or historical documents, the average person should understand some basic principles that will help preserve their own photographic heritage. Daylight and humidity are both threats to photographs. If you have questions about the proper methods of storage and display, consult a local museum or historical society for advice. Most important, don't just leave your pictures in a drawer or shoebox, take them out and enjoy them as much as possible.

1 Steven Marshall works only in enamel on glass and uses layers of glass in order to obtain the amazing effect of depth and shadow in his paintings. This is "P.O.V." There also seem to be layers of narrative in the painting—the perfect painting for observing life.

2 "Coco Hendaye, 1934" by Jacques Henri Lartigue (1894–1986) from a posthumous limited edition collection of platinum prints issued by the Ministère de la Culture—France/AAJHL. It has been said that Lartigue had "the ability to find joy in the 'every day'." I would also say that his ability to evoke the atmosphere of the world he photographed was—and still is—quite remarkable. This posthumous production enables collectors to purchase superb quality prints by Studio 31 of 35 of Lartigue's most celebrated images.

Suggested reading:

One Man's Eye by Alan Siegel

Three Seconds of Eternity by Robert Doisneau

Street Life in London by John Thomson and Adolphe Smith

Eugene Atget: Paris

2

Art and Architecture

The enormous and ever-growing interest in the home and the "comfort factor" has spawned myriad stores whose designers are household names. Television programs on interior design are shown almost every night, and in every color supplement of every weekend newspaper there will be several articles about the home, a new interior designer, or a furniture maker. On any newsstand the number of magazines with the words "house," "home," or "casa" in their title is beyond belief.

It is therefore not surprising that the same people who love their homes and who read these magazines so avidly would also show an interest in the paintings or photographs that show interior or even exterior scenes. Paintings of beautiful household objects, too, fall into this fascinating field.

For some people it is the domesticity of a painting of tea about to be served in the nineteenth century, for others it is the depiction of a corner of a room in someone else's home, yet others might yearn for a large exterior of a skyscraper in New York.

Our fascination for the home—whether bricks, mortar, and buildings or interiors—seems to translate into an equally fascinating love of the depiction of these things.

1 "Son of the Earth" by Bea Last, oil on canvas. This English artist's abstract oils are wonderful in contemporary minimal decoration. Her oils are warm and earthy as well as abstract, and they add an interesting mellow aspect to cool rooms.

2 "The Cross," New York city 1966, by Ernst Haas. All skyline views of New York are wonderful to me—and I believe to many other people. This, however, has to be one of the most special. The tops of the buildings are hidden by early evening mist, and the result is that, viewed from below, the mist forms a cross between the buildings. This would make a wonderful starting point for a collection of New York skyline views.

3 "The Picture Gallery" by David Connell. An extremely fine, detailed watercolor of a room with no other purpose than to house art. Connell is a master at interiors and often uses an existing room that he "fills" with the correct paintings and furniture. The detail is astonishing, and his work is treasured by collectors worldwide.

1 A magnificent pair of nine-teenth-century French iron gates. Architectural details and façades from the nineteenth century, particularly French, are much collected for their great detail as well as enormous artistic impact. The late Bill Blass had a wonderful collection.

2 "Rio Della Frescado" by Sandra Russell Clark. From a series entitled 'Venice: A Vanishing Light' (1992–1993). Art historian Edward Lucie Smith feels that New Orleans is the only city in the United States to bear a subtle and elusive resemblance to Venice. It is therefore understandable that New Orleans-based photographer Sandra Russell Clark was drawn to photograph Venice: both cities are "living on borrowed time." I discovered her work reading an article about the mysterious quality of Southern photography.

Buildings

I have long known that I am a "street person." By this I mean that, unlike most people, I am really not comfortable in the country or in small villages and hamlets. However, put me down in any large city and I am happy. It matters not that I may not speak a word of the language or know my way about—I am at home. It is therefore not surprising that I find Beaux Art watercolors of French buildings beautiful; that striking photographs of skyscrapers appeal or that I have long collected—and in fact frequently show in my gallery—watercolors of interiors both old and new.

It is, however, good to know that I am not alone and that artists for centuries have revelled in depicting the new buildings of their age at every level. Many people collect architectural watercolors and drawings, and framed and hung as a collection they are quite stunning as well as having great academic appeal. Good early items are no longer easy to find, but one can still happen upon very attractive, slightly later architectural drawings and watercolors to collect and hang. I have also discovered that the art of the interior is loved by many collectors, and historians as well, as it illustrates the details of a period long past.

Whereas I can accept that there is appeal to some of images of Highland cattle on Scottish moors or a ship on heavy seas or even a country garden, for me the view of the rooftops of Paris from a studio window beats the rural hands down.

Suggested reading:

New York Vertical by Horst Hamann

Photography and Architecture 1839–1939 by Richard Pare

Bernice Abbott: Changing New York edited by Bonnie Yochelson

The World of Atget by Eugene Atget and Bernice Abbott

3 "Suspension Wires" (circa 1955). This graphic photograph of the Brooklyn Bridge, New York shows the steel wires that suspend the roadbed. Engineer John Roebling designed the bridge. This is a really dramatic and different image showing the skyline of New York.

4 I could not resist another of Horst Hamann's powerful images of the New York skyline. Again this is an image from the series "New York Vertical," an interesting and instructive hint is that Hamann's images look even more wonderful if purchased in a very large format.

3

1 Thierry Bosquet's watercolor could only be Venice: and it is easy to see why more people seem drawn to images of Venice than any other city. Although painted in the 1990s, it could be Venice over 100 years ago.
It is for this ageless quality that Venice is so collected.

2 A classic façade of a French school building from the turn of the century, circa 1900. These watercolor architectural façades can still be found in France and, well framed and hung, can work wonderfully well as a mosaic wall of many different shapes and sizes of architectural images and details from all periods. This is, however, when one needs the services of a really good framer and picture hanger; this would be an easier wall to collect than to hang.

3 I feel I should call this "Heat and Dust" after the wonderful movie about India since that is the emotion it evokes. The artist, Scott, was in India in the 1880s. The painting is of the Purana Quila in Delhi. Today it is filled with people and the peace of this scene seems almost impossible.

2

1 A fine early nineteenth-century drawing of a bridge. It is interesting to note that paintings, drawings, and prints in this sort of shape are very desirable on a wall. They can add another layer, another dimension, to a group of more rectangular pictures.

2 This watercolor of an architectural detail in sanguine illustrates a perfect picture to add to a wall of architectural vistas old or new. The addition of close-up detail is a really stylish way to "change the pace" and give a wall an interesting spectrum of shape and size.

3 "Spiral Stairwell" by Raymond Kleboe. This photograph is of the main spiral stairwell at Queen's House, Greenwich, London. Seen from this angle, the stairwell forms a magnificent pattern and gives a really dramatic effect to this architectural image.

2

1

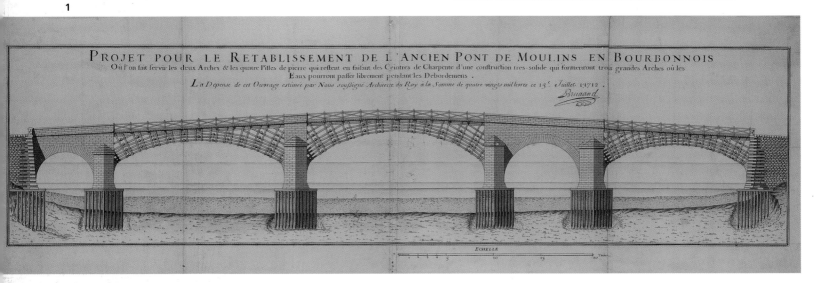

The beauty of buildings

Piers Gough
Leading London architect

In architecture, the main things are the buildings. Equally important, however, for the architects' immortality, are representations of those buildings. But before all that, they need to persuade people to build, or let them build, the buildings in the first place. The methods of persuasion are myriad. There are sketches, drawings and plans, sections and elevations, axonometric views, sketch models, finished models, and computer-generated walk-throughs. Then come sketches of details, before detailed technical drawings.

All these representations can be beautiful in their own right. With the exception of young or small firms, the hand of the actual named architect is liable to only be on the sketches or sketch models. The other presentation material is the result of collaboration with others in the team and/or representation specialists. In the past (before planning committees, etc.), this stuff could be emotional and exciting as well as stiff and abstract. Nowadays people demand the chimera of objective veracity, and the representation tends toward the coolly superreal—like demanding photographs before the event.

All these models of representation have their stars: from the heroic expressionist sketches of Eric Mendelson to the sublime paintings of J. M. Gandy, including famously and all too presciently Soane's great Bank of England in ruins. From Frank Gehry's many spectacular development models for each project to high-tech working drawings, there are wonderful examples of every sort.

Lutyens was one of the first architects, however, to become famous through the other great medium of representation: photography of the buildings themselves. For him, it was *Country Life* magazine that published his work assiduously and in depth. Now this medium is the main one for architectural representation and hence architectural discourse and, of course, fame. A whole profession of exclusively architectural photographers has grown up to capture seductively the architects' oeuvre, and these photographs can also be very beautiful in their own right.

However, in the end, there really is nothing better than the real things: the buildings themselves. Why not buy one today?

1 A collection of cigar cases, boxes, and a clock. A very masculine painting of items on a gentleman's hall table by Henry Koehler. I chose this painting mainly because it was so masculine in what is often essentially a very feminine area of collecting.

2 Paintings of china have always been very collectible. In this case, Galley has painted cups piled one upon the other: antique china but stacked in a very modern way. It is from a collection called "Cups and Saucers."

3 The interior paintings of Anne-Françoise Couloumy are collected by those of us who love interiors on both sides of the Atlantic. Couloumy's are very different—they are often rooms that are studios or strangely shaped. This painting is "Le Café New Yorkais."

4 "Salon Huis van Loon," Amsterdam 1998, by Alec Cobbe, from an exhibition at Rafael Valls Limited, London entitled "Alec Cobbe At Home and Abroad."

Interiors, Furniture, and Objects

I have always collected watercolor interiors and for many years have had annual exhibitions of interiors by several very good contemporary artists in my gallery. Peeking into the rooms and lives of other people is irresistible, and the particular genre of interiors that I have always found most appealing is the finely detailed, almost miniaturist, approach.

There is a wonderful book published by Franco Maria Ricci detailing and illustrating the superb interiors painted by the wonderful Russian designer, Alexandre Serebriakoff. It perfectly illustrates this delightful and very detailed look as well as demonstrating how fascinating historically and socially it can be to examine these paintings. Serebriakoff painted homes all over Europe.

This is not a genre that is newly fashionable; the great Mario Praz wrote *An Illustrated History of Interior Decoration: From Pompeii to Art Nouveau* in 1964, and his magnificent work is still the greatest reference on the subject. Subsequently, Stephen Calloway and Charlotte Gere wrote excellent books on the subject of interior paintings.

There is an intimacy in interior paintings that is very appealing, and these types of picture often look wonderful in a kitchen or dining room. As this area of the home becomes more of a focal point for family and friends, it becomes more and more important to have welcoming and appropriate art on the walls. I have always particularly loved paintings of paintings on the walls of a room, a picture gallery, a hall, and find these images quite ravishing.

3

4

5 Isabelle Rey's rooms are perfect, immaculate, pristine, and quite beautiful. The amount of detail Rey manages to incorporate beggars belief. This is a bedroom that has been furnished in a *toile de jouy*, and Rey has managed to capture every detail of color and pattern.

5

1 One of a series of six seriographs by Michel Lablais,
each of a Chinese chair and
each with a different object
or piece of fabric on or
around the chair. It can be
very chic to have a three-
above-three effect with six
almost identical pictures.

2 This enchanting watercolor
of a bathroom is by David
Connell, the American interi-
or artist. Bathrooms are
surprisingly popular but not
easy to find, so the exhibition we did of bathroom
paintings some years ago
was a sellout.

On interiors

Min Hogg
Founder and editor of The World of Interiors

Show me the man whose quality of life is
not affected for good or ill by his surroundings. Everybody alive responds
favorably to aesthetic harmony, even if
they haven't a clue as to the reason why.
From the very first designs dabbed onto a
cave wall, man's basic instinct has been to
beautify his home.

Astonishingly, there are also many in
whom this basic instinct is deeply buried,
but that is probably just as well—other-
wise, there would be no need for interior
decorators. Nor would there be scope for
those like myself who have an urge to
share their passion for all things beautiful
or decorative with as many people as possible, finding expression in my case by
editing *The World of Interiors* magazine
for twenty years.

I had no idea I was so evangelical on
my subject until I began that magazine,
nor quite how important good decoration can be to one's wellbeing. Having
been brought up among beautiful things,
living in a household where the choice of
a new upholstery fabric, or the purchase
of a new picture—be it expensive or
cheap—was a delicious matter of life and

death to my mother, that was my norm,
it never occurred to me that there might
be people who needed awakening to the
joys involved in designing and decorating
an interior.

Putting together a room has remained
one of life's major pleasures for me. The
agony of it is still every bit as exquisite as
it was in my mother's day, and since I go
along with Voltaire's declaration that
originality is nothing but judicious pla-
giarism, I don't stint myself when it
comes to snooping at—and borrowing
from—the collecting and decorating solu-
tions of others.

Naturally, I devour all the house and
home magazines, shameless in my
voyeurism, but perhaps the greatest
source of inspiration comes from the
study of paintings depicting interiors.
There is something unique about a wonderful room captured by an artist, in
watercolor or oils, that is far more
descriptive and heart-rending than a
photograph can ever be. There is a precious gemlike quality to them that makes
one ache to possess such pictures.

Maybe one should have a frisson of
guilt at peeping uninvited into the painted world of complete strangers, but
never let that prevent you from borrowing all the best decorating ideas.

Suggested reading:

*An Illustrated History of Interior Decoration:
From Pompeii to Art Nouveau* by Mario Praz

A Book of Books by Abelardo Morell

3 A dramatic corner of a very grand palazzo by Thierry Bosquet, like a moment from one of the operas he designs for opera houses around the world. Lavish silk, so real one can feel it, and elaborate furnishings feature in a grand moment from ages past.

4 An artist's studio, probably in Paris, circa 1900, by E. de Closets. Just looking at this page you can see how well the many fields of interiors go together and show how this can be an open-ended collection. The best collections are ones that take a long time to amass and are never finished. Just when you think you have everything you need, you see another item you have to have, or you find you want to move a picture to another room and the whole search begins again – and that is the fun of it all.

4

1 and 2 Manufacturers' pattern books have long been a source of interesting pictures. By the middle of the nineteenth century they were printed in color, as was the sample book from which these magnificent plates of paintbrushes came. They are quite astonishingly linear

and modern, and page after page showed different brushes for different trades and work. These are harder and harder to find today but the Museum Carnevale in Paris has a great collection and has published a book of trade catalogs.

3 Another page from a trade catalog that made a dramatic picture in an elegant kitchen/dining room. This time the illustrations were of fine silverware. Such well-known companies as Christofle and Baccarat all had fine trade catalogs of this sort.

4 "Pale Vessels III" by G from a series in which empty vessels are grouped in pale colors, in a gentle yet very memorable way. I love these soft colors—they work so well in the northern hemisphere where the light is soft and we do not often have a great deal of natural light.

5 Desiree Dolron's pictures are unlike anything I have seen in contemporary photography. They are arresting, beautiful, political, and mesmerizing. The scale is monumental, and they need to be seen close up. This is a school library in Cuba—an enchanting image.

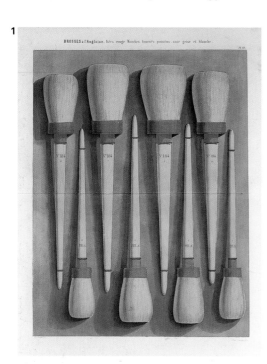

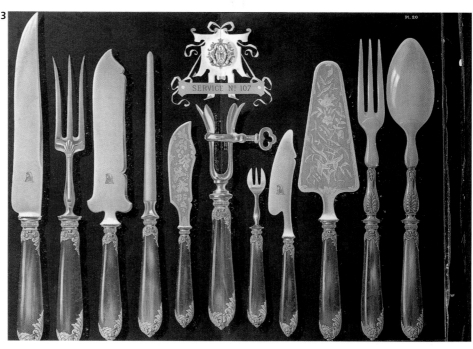

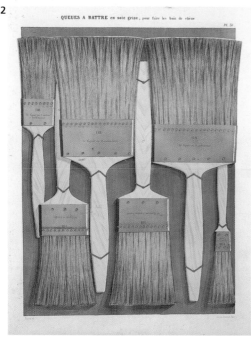

1 "Open Dictionary" by Abelardo Morell, 2001, silver gelatin print. For those of us who love books as objects as well as literature and reading matter, Morell's title, *A Book of Books*, with a divine selection of photographs celebrating every aspect of the beauty of books, will be a treat for the eyes and soul. Morell's work is sensitive, finely textured, and very moving. I like the thought of this photograph on a wall with pictures of rooms—or more specifically libraries.

2 This formal settee is an eighteenth-century design for an English settle, but made in the nineteenth century by an English furnituremaker. This watercolor came from the archive of the company when it was dissolved in the early years of the twentieth century. Such watercolors were done by artists and artisans working for the firm to show clients what their ordered piece of furniture would look like. They are much sought after by collectors.

1

3 Photorealism seems to have returned to popularity in this new century, and many artists can be found who work in this way. Stewart Brown's oil is very different to everything else here and would not go with more traditional art, but would be good to hang in a casual environment.

4 Another oil by Stewart Brown, showing everyday objects in a very mundane way, but with great charm and humor. Brown works in oil and caseine on canvas, and juxtaposes interesting and unusual elements in his paintings. "Chair with Panama Hat and Cane," 2003, was one of a series of chair paintings we showed in our gallery last year, and they all sold very quickly. Chairs have always been popular—have you noticed how Van Gogh's yellow chair is always the image they choose to put on a poster!

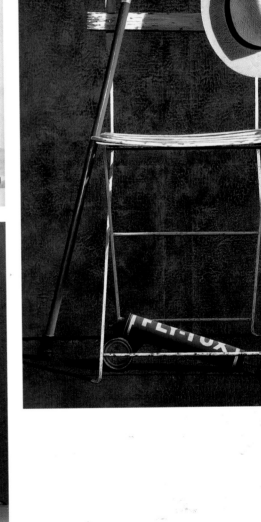

1 A shipping box by Louis Boudreault. These boxes reflect the way in which the colors that were used to create the masterpieces of Western painting were procured during the Renaissance. Curiously, the color road would often cross the spice road. Boudreault writes, "Imagine for a moment these boxes of color, expected for months, coming full of dreams from their country of origin." I have loved these boxes of pigment from the moment I first saw them.

2 "Waves III" by McDermott. Large sheets of handmade paper have been cut and attached to a Lucite back. The ever-changing effect of the paper is apparent in different light and adds a wonderful texture to a minimal contemporary room.

3 Neil Reddy creates images by recording the tracks, pulses, and flares that light makes inside the camera as it travels across the negative. His images are abstract, but also an explanation of the photographic process.

4 Another example of the effective use of stripes, in this case by Chris Gallagher. We illustrate "Quake" (2000), oil on canvas. He lays down one striation of color after another to gain this amazing effect, which is oddly comforting and comprehensible.

Abstracts

Abstract art seems to me a very personal thing. Twenty people can look at the same painting and each one will see something totally different— and the variety of opinion can be enormous. I suspect that the inspirations for abstract art are different to those for representational art, being moodier and dreamier. Once one knows what the artist had in his mind it is, of course, a lot easier to distinguish the sensation, emotion, or theme he is describing; but when one looks unschooled, so to speak, the range of images that can appear in one's mind, is vast.

I believe that the marvelous "stripes" of the famed Bridget Riley have influenced people enormously as again and again I am seeing work that seems very much to have been inspired by her unique talent. I marvel at the enormous range of feeling that can exist in the varying

widths and colors and depths of these stripes. The effect is both astonishing, beautiful, and strangely calming. I find the concept of the stripe
returned to more and more in abstract art, to very pleasing effect.

It is always hard for a strictly figurative person like myself to write
convincingly about abstract art. From my choice of images for this section, it must be apparent that I need to have something linear, some
form of texture, some sort of strength in order to be able to react at all.
Perhaps what I have chosen would not be considered abstract by everyone, but it is as abstract as I can be.

Suggested reading:

John Heartfield: Aiz:VI 1930–38

Photomontage by Dawn Ades

The Essential Mark Rothko by Klaus Ottmann

Adam Fuss by Adam Fuss and Eugenia Parry

1 "York Peppermint Pattie" by Jonathan Lewis (2001). From the series "See Candy." These are a limited edition of iris prints.

2 Bea Last's vertical striped oil on canvas continues with this feeling of line and color that I find so appealing for today. This painting is called "Yellow Earth No. 2."

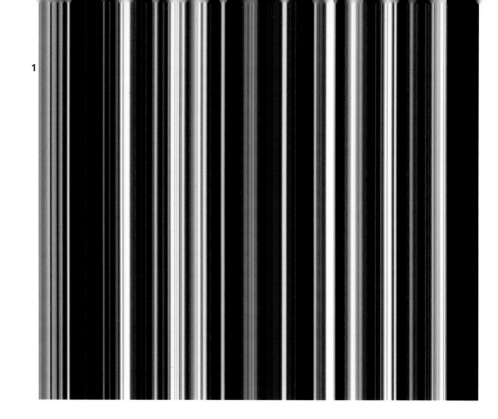

1

Abstract inspiration

Jonathan Lewis
Abstract photographer

The series of See Candy prints was inspired by a box of chocolates that I was given. There's a company in San Francisco called See's Candy that not only makes delicious chocolates, but also puts them into dandy little boxes. I kept the box and had the idea of distorting photos of candy wrappers to the extent that you couldn't see them but your brain could. I made 47 tiny pictures, each of a different candy—all the way from Almond Joy through Milky Way to York Peppermint Pattie—and put them in the box.

Visually the stripes are fun, but some people have noticed a dark undercurrent of futuristic barcode hell, and I like that, too. You could say they were about commercialism, consumerism, and advertising, but mostly they are about finding beauty in unlikely places. Candy wrappers don't have much going for them aesthetically, but shine a bright light on them and the crinkles open up a whole spectrum of unexpected colors.

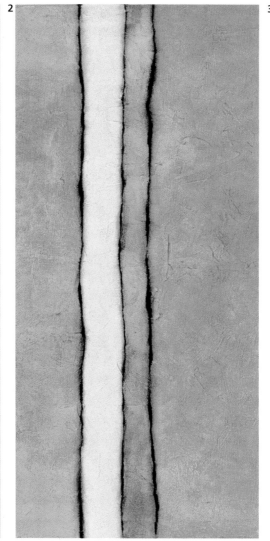

2

3

4

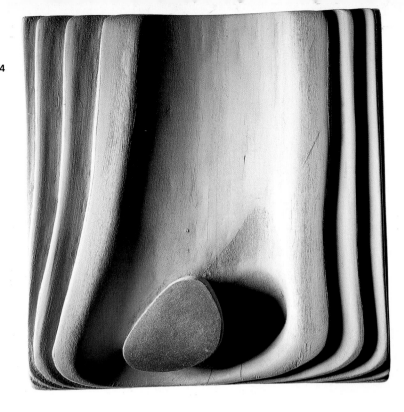

3 Thierry Flon, a Belgian architect, paints in oil on canvas, and though totally abstract there is, nevertheless, the definition of form within his work. He uses only shades of black, gray, and white, yet seems to find many tones in these non-colors.

4 Amanda Dow Thompson's carved wood linear piece is untitled and strongly graphic. I love using art that is three-dimensional together with paintings and photography. I think that the contrast gives emphasis to both mediums.

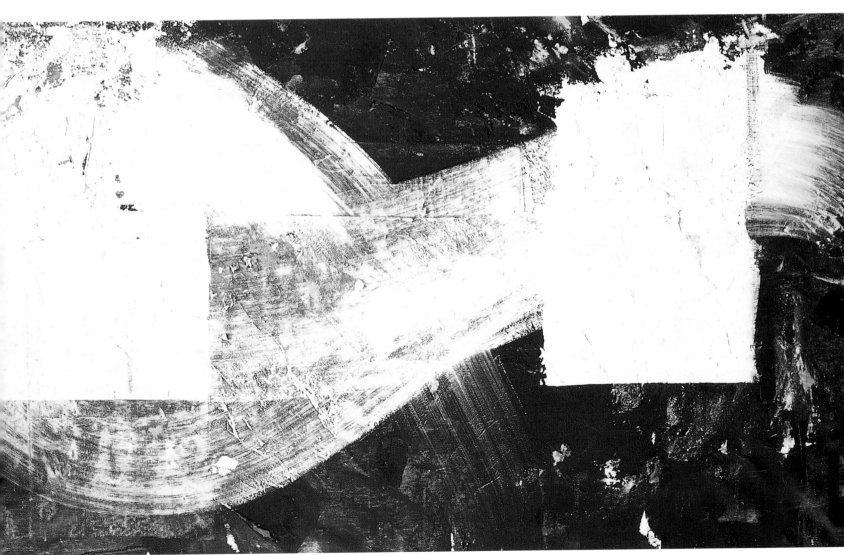

The Natural World

The natural world has attracted more artists than any other area over the centuries. Flowers, landscape, seascape, animals: these are the subjects that have been painted since painting began.

It is not difficult to understand this; before buildings of any substance were built, nature reigned supreme, and everyone was inspired in one way or another by what was around them as they lived and worked. Even religious paintings tended to have vast amounts of landscape around them, often with biblical scenes reenacted in Tuscan or Lombard scenery. The natural world was calming, beautiful, serene, and inspiring.

In today's quite different world these subjects remain constantly popular with artists, photographers, and collectors. Possibly the reasons are the same, even though we no longer live in a peaceful world, nor do most of us see much of the natural world around us. Perhaps this makes the natural world even more beautiful to us all in the twenty-first century.

2

3

4

1 Beach huts were part of my childhood and somehow they represent nostalgia and the happiest times of my youth. Every time I see one, I think of Cape Town and long summers. This oil painting by Jane Hewlett makes me think of Norfolk and not-so-warm summers but is very evocative of my childhood. Nostalgia has a large place in buying art for one's home—and so it should.

2 "Blue Poppy" by Tessa Traeger. A piezo pigment print in an edition of 18 signed and numbered.

3 "Polar Bears" by Britta Jaschinski, silver gelatin print, available from the artist.

4 "Seahorse, *Hippocampus erectus*," by Henry Horenstein from the series and book *Aquatics*, platinum print.

1 From "In Search of Eden," a work that chronicled Sandra Russell Clark's search for her own Eden, culminating in her moving to a small Mississippi coastal town. The lushness and sensuality of the South is evoked in these mysterious photographs, as well as a feeling of myth and history.

2 "Summer Haze, South Hams" by Stephen Brown RBA. The paintings I have seen by this artist have all had a sensation of high sky, as does this one. It is an alluring vision of long summer days in the country, executed with great feeling and somehow very English.

3 To say that the magnificent, large photographs by David Parker are extraordinary would be an understatement. Parker uses a custom-made panoramic camera and high-definition military reconnaissance film. This is how he manages to get such extraordinary depth and

Land and Seascapes

This has always been an extremely popular field of art, with town dwellers lusting after the Scottish Highlands and Tuscan hills. In turn, collectors living in apartments in landlocked cities yearn for the sight and sound of the sea. Peaceful men long for heavy seas, and I, for one, have a longing for beach paintings à la Boudin's paintings of the North Atlantic French coast of Normandy and Brittany.

In my case I suspect it is a throwback to an idyllic childhood in Cape Town, where we grew up knowing how to swim in the sea and spent all the time possible at the beach. I grew up with the sound of the Atlantic Ocean in my ears and sand between my toes, as they say! We also had a blue painted beach hut, as did most people we knew in those days, and so I am always drawn to any painting that shows "bathing boxes".

The images in this chapter are breathtaking: from the mysterious, ethereal photography of Sandra Russell Clark to the evocative paintings of Sarah Carrington. The artists and photographers each take their own approach to celebrating their surroundings, and the diversity of the resulting images is striking, perhaps more so here than for any other subject covered in this chapter.

1

2

Suggested reading:

Ansel Adams at 100

Open Skies by Don McCullin

Water's Edge by Harry M. Callahan

David Parker: The Phenomenal World

Hiroshi Sugimoto: Seascapes

detail into his glorious land-scapes. The printing is toned silver gelatin and the size is 67 ¾" x 39 ¾". The impact of first seeing a Parker land-scape is almost physical and one never forgets this sensa-tion. You *have* to see the real thing.

4 "Yuma Desert" (1996) by Ken Griffiths, platinum print. Griffiths' photograph perfectly evokes the drama and visual impact of the desert land-scape. One can imagine getting lost in this image.

5 This Provençal painting by Luce Géas is full of energy and mirrors the intensity of the colors of the region. Géas moved from painting seascapes to landscapes, and her palette changed to one of great vibrancy.

5

3

4

1 "Clouds over Yosemite" by Bob Kolbrener. Kolbrener writes that the Yosemite experience continues to be the cornerstone for all of his western excursions. He feels that the inherent qualities of space, scale, and quietude of the Great American West are all amplified in Yosemite National Park.

2 "Facing the Horizon IV" by Marco Crivello, Dutch silver leaf and oil on board. This large, abstract landscape is moody and beautiful in a somber, brooding sense.

2

1

Landscape seascape

Bonni Benrubi
Dealer in contemporary photography

Since 1855 when the photograph was born, man has always wanted to record and present the great vistas of nature, the landscape, and the sea. These images were records of a world near to us and also a record of a world far, far away—one we could only dream about.

In the mid-nineteenth century, landscape and ocean photographs were primarily made as records of a place. Work was often commissioned and funded by a government or a private individual. (T. H. O'Sullivan's work for the US Geographical Survey of the American West is an example.) Also, graphs were souvenirs of a visit—remember, people didn't own cameras as

they do today. These pictures were pasted into scrapbooks or displayed on walls.

Early on, cameras were cumbersome and required long exposures. But the photographs created were pristine and beautiful works of art—the predecessors and inspiration for modern and contemporary artists. From Gustave Le Gray's haunting seascapes of the nineteenth century to Ansel Adams' immaculate Western views and Hiroshi Sugimoto's spare and quiet compositions today, the landscape and seascape remain subjects true to the heart and soul of life.

Simple, relatively inexpensive, anonymous views can be found on the internet, in flea markets, secondhand shops, even garage sales. With a nice oversized mat and frame, you can have an original work of art for very little money. As one

enters the world of "fine art" looking for landscapes or seascapes, the approach is different but equally plentiful. Exquisitely crafted, mural-size images made in exotic materials such as platinum and gold, as well as views by blue-chip and emerging photographers, can be found on the internet, in art galleries, and at auction houses. You can find great deals on blue-chip material at charity events and auctions. Remember when traveling that there are often local galleries and shops that can offer you images for sale.

Research the pricing of fine art images and be aware that factors such as signature and condition are vital. For less expensive, anonymous, and unknown views, go with your instincts and weigh the level of pleasure an image can command against the cost.

3

3 "Sea Fence" by Noel Myles. Myles assembles his pictures from dozens of separate negatives to evoke the experience of a place rather than a momentary view of it. He liberates his stills from static. His work seems to bridge the gap between photography and painting.

4 Mixed media painting by Sarah Carrington entitled "Summer Clouds, North End, Iona." Again and again, one realizes the allure of sea and landscape: they add a quality of peace and sanity to our all too hectic lives.

4

1 and 2 From "Gardens of Reflection" by Sandra Russell Clark, 1985–89. Clark is best known for her images of gardens and mysterious landscapes. "Villandry France" (1) and "Isola Bella" (2) are both from this series and are both exquisite images of gardens seen through the eyes of Clark. The photographs in this collection are in an edition of 50 and can be purchased in a large size enabling one to see the great detail and sensuality that Clark brings to her work.

3 Maureen Jordan's paintings epitomize an idealized sense of an English garden. Sadly not all gardens look like Jordan's, she works in pastel and uses the medium to give subtle definition and shading to the colors of her garden.

4 Isabelle Rey paints French gardens in her miniaturist style. Her detail is extraordinary, and her gardens are always more finely groomed than the English version. Her paintings are small and very precious with each and every flower head perfectly painted.

Gardens

Depictions of gardens have always been extremely popular. Ever since the concept of a garden (as opposed to countryside) arose, people have enjoyed seeing reproductions of them hung on a wall.

Gardens have changed in their design and popularity since the first, very formal Dutch gardens, and the mode today is for something far more natural and less structured than even 20 years ago. This change is paralleled by the changing style of garden paintings. The very early ones tended to be formal and lacking in spontaneity. In the late nineteenth and early twentieth centuries, paintings of cottage gardens were very much in vogue, and such artists as Beatrice Parsons depicted them with accuracy and great charm. Today, however, although garden paintings still exist and are sought after, they tend to be more abstract and flowing, full of wondrous color and movement rather than being perfectly formed and synchronized.

Gardens of reflection

Sandra Russell Clark
Photographer

I have always been drawn to ethereal landscapes, whether they are natural or gardens created by man as sanctuaries, which serve no other purpose than to delight. When photographing for "Gardens of Reflection," I wanted to emphasize the fanciful and otherworldly quality of the gardens. In using infrared film and subtle hand-coloring, I brought a surreal quality to the photographs, a dreamy counterpoint to the precise composition of the images.

3

4

Suggested reading:

A Gardener's Labyrinth: Portraits of People, Plants and Places by Tessa Traeger and Patrick Kinmonth

English Cottage Gardens by Edwin Smith

Atget's Gardens by Eugene Atget

The Gardens at Giverny: A View of Monet's World by Stephen Shore

1 Penny White's flower paintings have an academic, botanical, and natural history sense to them as well as great beauty. This large painting of poppies illustrates many different versions and types of poppy, giving us great detail individually, but also great beauty as a whole.

2 "Au Jardin" by Louis Lemaire, oil on canvas. This romantic painting is in complete contrast to the Zoe Hersey alongside it showing a different spirit from a more leisurely age.

Flowers and Botanicals

I started my career in Walton Street, London, and at the Winter Antique Show in New York by presenting the art of botanical illustration as it had not been shown before. I found ways of framing and mounting flowers that brought them from the bedrooms of old houses into the drawing rooms and dining rooms of the '80s and '90s. Such seventeenth-century masters as Basil Besler and Crispin de Passe became as well known to ladies who were decorating their homes and walls as the names of well-known novelists.

There will always be a love of flowers, and their depiction will be a constant delight to generations to come. However, it is no longer just oil, watercolor, gouache, and engraving. Today there is a generation of superb and talented photographers who bring a totally new aspect to this art form. In many cases they are gardeners as well as photographers of flowers, as were their predecessors in the world of floral painting.

Whether you prefer one medium or another, it is hard not to be moved by the image of a flower. Often it is the depiction of one glorious moment in a short life span, and this ephemeral moment becomes captured forever on one's wall.

Suggested reading:

Karl Blossfeldt: 1865–1932 by Karl Blossfeldt

Imogen Cunningham: Flora by Richard Lorenze

Flower Portraits by Joyce Tenneson

Flowers by Robert Mapplethorpe

One Hundred Flowers by Harold Feinstein

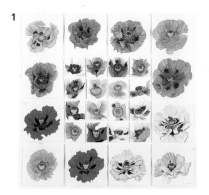

3 This large painting of flowers by Zoe Hersey of Atlanta has an almost Zenlike quality about it. I chose it for this sense of peace, which was quite different to any of the other flower paintings we have illustrated. I find her work most appealing.

3

1 "Pansies in Terracotta Pots" by Meg McCarthy. I have always loved paintings of flowers in pots—especially old pots that have a feeling of moss or cracking on them. McCarthy did an entire show for us once, and we filled the gallery with this informal garden feel.

2 "Green Cabbage in Pot" is also by McCarthy. As ornamental cabbages have become more popular in window boxes in London and elsewhere, they have become much desired in paintings as well.

3 A hand-colored engraving by J. Weinmann, 1767, in original color. Hand-colored engravings of flowers have long been desired and collected. Weinmann's epic work illustrated almost all the flora known to naturalists in the mid-eighteenth century.

4 "White Arums" by Galley from a series called simply "White Flowers." Galley painted a large series of white flowers, in jugs, vases, and pots, to celebrate the publication of my *White on White* book.

2

3

4

GALLEY. 2000.

5 "Flowers in a Pot" by Jules-Fréderic Ballavoine—a study taken from a larger painting. White flowers are, I believe, the favorite flowers of most women; they have certainly been popular in the gallery.

6 Maureen Jordan painted these spring flowers in pots in her potting shed—though naturalistic in its grouping, this painting in pastels is nonetheless decorative and appealing. Once again, a very English painting.

French flower paintings

Michael Brookstone
of Julian Simon Fine Art

The ever-popular genre of French flower painting is still one of the most effective types of painting to use in room decoration. Because of the inventive use of color, these paintings are marvelous instruments for harmonizing and coordinating the elements of a room setting.

The beginning of the nineteenth century saw the rise of the Romantic movement, which rejected the traditional and gave way to a freedom of painting in composition, use of texture and paint, as yet unexplored. No longer were paintings of flowers a traditional catalog of bulbs, blooms, and formal set arrangements; a new, exciting, and adventurous style was developing. New schools of flower painters flourished and were centered in Lyon and Dijon.

As a result of the influence of, among others, Delacroix and Courbet, artists depicted the sense of a flower rather than a detailed rendering of its shape, color, and texture. The Impressionist movement that started in the 1860s, of course, had an enormous impact.

Some of the most charming and desirable of these pictures are simplified studies of flowers not in grand surroundings, but cut, in baskets and occasionally growing. In most of these paintings, the pots and vases are underplayed and subsidiary to the sense of the flower. The language of flowers flourished, with each bloom and leaf having a symbolic meaning, for example, violets for modesty, myrtle for passion, daisy for innocence, cornflower for delicacy, bay for glory, ferns for fascination, and pansies for thoughtfulness.

The continuity of the genre of flower and still-life painting meant that it encompassed all the major artistic movements of the twentieth century, from Post-Impressionism (e.g., Van Gogh, Seurat, Cézanne) through to Cubism, Picasso, Surrealism, Magritte, and beyond. Watercolors and oils in all sizes—from the most serious and academic, to the frivolous and decorative, from the bizarre to the enchanting—all exist in this genre.

Although many schools of painting existed in France, that of French flower painting has always played an important part and is undeniably unique. It is still possible to find fine, affordable examples of all schools of French flower painting.

New Botanicals

1 and 2 When I first started work on this book, the initial interview I did was with Ron Van Dongen. I had quite fallen in love with his photography of flowers. It was at that moment that I thought that this was the new botanical imagery—not any longer the watercolored and printed image of earlier years but new, exciting, detailed, and very beautiful reality. The four colors of roses were always going to be the opening page for this section. Van Dongen's work is ethereal, spiritual, and yet the work of a true gardener. He is a perfectionist in his gardening and photography. 1. *Fritillaria meleagris* 2. (clockwise from top left) *Rosa* Black Beauty; *Rosa* "Leonidas II"; *Rosa* "Grace de Monaco"; *Rosa* "Meinivoz Summers Kiss."

Photographing flowers

Ron Van Dongen
Flower photographer

"Nobody sees a flower, really; it is so small. We haven't time, and to see takes time—like to have a friend takes time."
Georgia O'Keefe

If I were able to translate images and events into words, I would certainly do that. It is a fact, however, that I understand the world around me in terms of what I see. The earliest memories from my living environment are those of plants, animals, the creek, and the garden. It would be hard for me to write down these memories, but the images are still clear in my head. As a child, I would spend most of my time outside, in the woods or on a nearby old farm. Eventually the garden became woven into my activities.

My first garden experiment was in a sandy corner underneath a rose bush, where I sowed radish seeds. The entire spring season I followed the development of that priceless piece of soil. Once the radishes were ready for harvest, I didn't know what to do, because I disliked the taste of them. The following year I tried my hand at marigolds. One can't imagine how proud I was of those plants.

In my development as a photographer, I followed the same rules as I did with that tiny corner of that first garden: I kept things simple and focused on one part of a whole. That was—and is—the only way I understand things. With every attempt to get a general overview, things go wrong. On the rare occasions when I tried to photograph landscapes, I felt completely lost; I saw too many things at once and I couldn't get close to my subject matter.

While attending photo school, one of my teachers suggested that, for a successful photo series, you don't have to look any farther than your backyard. That advice I have followed literally. Although it has never been my intention to photograph plants and flowers professionally, I consistently feel the urge to expose what is going on in the garden on film. I consider the plant "portraits" as garden documentation. It is a good way to look back at how everything develops. That sounds strange, because the final photographs show no details of the garden at all, but for me it is the right information. I consider it a visual journal.

The way I garden and approach photography go together well: I will be in the garden, futzing around in a small corner, for instance. There is already so much to see. If I find something interesting, I take it into the studio (also in the backyard) and continue my quest underneath the north-facing skylights. With the camera I am able to get even closer, and I discover that the plant and flower parts start to lead their own lives: a beauty you are likely to miss just strolling through the garden. Through the camera lens, the flowers look like independent beings, not parts of a plant. It is breathtaking.

Over the years, developing the garden and practicing photo skills have become a full-time job.

1

1 "Agave" by Ron Van Dongen. Van Dongen turns his lens to the plant from which we make tequila! I recommend the books and portfolios Van Dongen has produced (details on his website).

2 *Iris kaempferi* (Japanese iris)" by Judith McMillan. Using an X-ray machine as a camera, McMillan photographs the internal structure of plants, revealing the beauty of natural forms invisible to the human eye. Her images are eerie and beautiful. This is a toned silver gelatin print.

3 "Blushing Bride I" by Joyce Tenneson. From a series called "Flower Portraits— The Life Cycle of Beauty." Tenneson, a portait photographer, says that she sees flowers not as mere decorations, but as distinctive personalities.

4 "Parrot Tulips" by Bruce Rae. It has been written of Rae by Robin Muir that "his approach to photographing flowers suggests portraiture at its purest and most solitary." This seems very valid to me. His flowers are "masterpieces in miniature," another remark by Muir, which sums up these exquisite studies of flowers.

Animals

From the Noah's ark of one's childhood and all the images of A. A. Milne, most of us have always associated animals with well-loved pictures. Perhaps more than any other genre, it is with us from childhood to adolescence. From youth to maturity, images of animals symbolize all things to all men and women. It is, therefore, not surprising that animal painting and photography are eternally popular and always blend superbly with most other genres. They can be sophisticated, abstract or photo-real, savage or gentle. They are always well loved.

I have selected dogs as the only animal to warrant a separate section in the pages that follow. I know this will elicit cries of "unfair" from cat and horse lovers, from the "love thy donkey" league, and elephant, rabbit, and monkey aficionados. But it is my book and I could not include them all; the dog is, after all, considered to be man's best friend. The amount of literature and illustrated material on the subject also helped me make up my mind.

Like all of the portrait painters we have selected for that chapter, the artists in this section capture the spirit and personality of the particular animal rather than just painting a breed or type. This is especially apparent in the images of dogs I have chosen—the character of each is immediately obvious, and it is plain that the artists themselves have a great understanding of these wonderful animals. I think I loved best of all the quotation from Kafka, noted in Henry Horenstein's book, *Canine*: "All knowledge, the totality of all questions and answers is contained in the dog."

1 "Hedgehog" by Saverio Polloni, an Italian artist who excels in the field of super-realism. He is an animal artist extraordinaire, but with a difference: it is almost as if his animals are posing with every whisker groomed and intact: official portraits in a very stylistic way.

2 "The Bull" by Michael J. Austin is a glorious oil on canvas. It emerges strongly from its gilded background in an almost mythical fashion—yet this is a strong and real bull. It is such a contrast to all the other images on this spread.

3 The nineteenth-century watercolor of canaries and other songbirds is by an unknown artist. It is quite whimsical and was one of a pair. As I keep mentioning, these long narrow paintings are a boon to collectors who want to hang a medley of different shapes and sizes.

4 The "Horse, Rider and Hounds," by an unknown artist, is a typical, almost naïve, country painting. Country people wanted their favorite animals painted, and there were many artists who traveled the country doing just this.

5 The magnificent and regal tiger is also by Saverio Polloni, and once again take note of the shape of the painting: it can be wonderful to hang a tall narrow picture on a narrow wall, almost floor to ceiling, thus giving the room a much taller feel.

4

5

3

1 "Mountain Zebras" by Jonathan Comerford are extremely detailed drypoint etchings executed in a fine nineteenth-century way seldom ever used today in our world of digital imaging. One only has to look at them to know that these etchings are of the optimum quality.

2 "Rhinoceros" by Britta Jaschinski is a silver gelatin print, available from the artist. Contrast this detailed and striking photograph with the woodcut by Dürer. It is interesting to see how similar the two images are.

3 Henry Horenstein's "Brown Sea Nettle" is from the series and book entitled *Aquatics*. It is both specific and abstract, and has a really mesmerizing quality about it. Platinum Print.

4 This classical—and most famous—image of a rhinoceros is by Albrecht Dürer. The woodcut is from the sixteenth century, and is the most powerful image of the animal in existence. And it is not thought that Dürer had actually seen one.

Animals in art

David T. Schiff

Chairman, the Wildlife Conservation Society

Nature has always inspired our art, and no other aspect of nature has so intensely and consistently fired human creativity and imagination as the other species with which we share the earth, on land and at sea. Since the first "artists" drew mammoths, horses, boars, and bison on the walls of the Cave of Lascaux nearly 17,000 years ago, animals have moved us to make their images. And in those images, over the centuries, is represented the fundamental, complex, and often perplexing relationship we have with other creatures.

We have used images of animals to try to control a natural world that was daunting and unfathomable—our prehistoric ancestors created art as magic, drawing animals before a hunt in an attempt to assure success. We have transformed virtually every substance, from the wood of a Northwest-coast Native American totem pole to the gold of an Egyptian tomb, into potent animal images and symbols that define our myriad cultures and beliefs.

From ancient Sumerian artisans to contemporary Disney animation artists, we depict animals as people, and use what we see as the "best" and "worst" in animals to express the best or worst traits in ourselves. From early African art to the works of Rembrandt and Rubens, the lion has reigned as a universal symbol of power. In bronzes that depict life and death struggles between predator and prey, Barye grapples with the untamed fierceness that lies beneath the surface of civilized man. Bosch uses odd and ghastly amalgamations of species—nature gone horribly wrong—to populate his gothic images of Hell. The perfect melding of heavenly form and function that is the horse fascinated da Vinci in one century, and Stubbs in another; before both, a mythical horse inspired one of the greatest surviving works of art from the Middle Ages, the Unicorn Tapestries.

We are inexorably and enduringly drawn to animals. Before comfortable travel and television, wild species were dizzyingly exotic. Early European menageries and zoos provided the inspiration for countless artists, including the sculptor Bugatti. So great was the fascination, Dürer created his famous rhinoceros engraving without ever having seen such an animal; his work was based solely upon reports from an eyewitness who had seen one at the Royal Zoo in Lisbon.

Art bears out the place of wildlife in our psyche. But paintings, sculptures, and images will lose their potency should the subjects be lost forever. Would a Delacroix tiger—like the animal itself, an almost impossible combination of power and beauty—touch us as deeply if tigers, like dinosaurs, were no more? Who now remembers the passenger pigeon?

As stewards of this planet, we must go beyond being moved by images of animals and act to conserve our natural world. The abiding place of animals in art confirms their place in our hearts and minds, and that is the most promising sign for those of us who care deeply about the future of our fellow species.

Collecting dog paintings

William Secord
Dealer in canine paintings

There are few people whose lives have not been touched by the love of a dog, and, since the nineteenth century, this affection has been transformed into innumerable paintings.

Dog paintings have long been popular with purebred dog fanciers who, like those in the horse world, want portraits of their favorite breed, or better yet, an ancestor of the dogs they have today. Sportsmen continue to want depictions of pointers, setters, or spaniels at work in the field, and pet owners want paintings of their own canine companions.

Nineteenth-century dog paintings, and those that are created today, may be categorised in three groups: purebred, sporting, and pet. The purebred dog portrait became popular with the evolution of organized dog shows in the nineteenth century, with The Kennel Club in London and its American equivalent in New York. How a dog looked when it competed in the show ring became very important indeed, and artists such as Maud Earl, Arthur Wardle, and John Emms, among others, specialized in the depiction of purebred specimens. In the purebred dog portrait convention, the dog is posed in profile, feet firmly on the floor, with its head slightly turned toward the viewer.

Many of these artists also painted dogs in the field, continuing the eighteenth-century British sporting art tradition and creating wonderful paintings of working setters and pointers, or foxhounds running over the hunting field. The classic sporting-dog painting shows the dog on point, proudly posed with dead game, or rushing full speed across a field.

Perhaps the most popular genre of dog painting today is the pet portrait, in which the only thing of importance is the dog as a companion to man, whether pictured on a pillow in a lavishly decorated interior or sitting on a doorstep waiting for its master's return. Pet portraits are among the most collectible of dog paintings; many of my clients have contemporary or Impressionist paintings in the living room, but they have pet portraits in the den or the library.

Whether you collect head studies that are grouped together up a staircase, or go for the major impact of one large painting, these friendly companions from the past can add inviting warmth to a room that can be achieved no other way. I have clients who collect paintings by only one artist, only nineteenth-century head studies or even paintings only of black dogs, because they remind them of a favorite pet. Many people collect paintings of only one breed, as did the late Marie A. Moore, who had over 300 depictions of Old English mastiffs, all now in the American Kennel Club Museum of the Dog in Saint Louis. Increasingly, like their nineteenth-century counterparts, modern pet owners commission portraits of their own beloved pets.

Photographs may re-create the physical appearance of a dog, but a fine painting goes beyond mere anatomy, capturing the true personality and spirit of our canine companions.

4 "Oreo, Popcorn and Licorice" by Charlotte Sorré, oil on canvas. Sorré studied in California and has become one of the most celebrated dog and horse portrait painters in the country.

5 "Boss T" by Peter Clark. One of a series of mixed media works by the artist that is full of humor and attitude.

1

2

3

1 "Poodle and Chauffeur" by Thurston Hopkins, c. 1950. An amusing and evocative scene of a poodle being taken for a drive, and both poodle and driver taking the situation very seriously.

2 Christine Merrill has a host of satisfied clients throughout the United States. Her paintings of dogs are traditional, using age-old techniques, and these portraits bring pleasure to dog owners everywhere. This King Charles spaniel is oil on canvas.

3 "Dalmation," London, by an unknown artist. A Dalmatian sticks his head outside one of the judging pens at Crufts Dog Show in London 1974.

4 Oil painting of a French bulldog by François Bard. Bard's strong brushwork and simple images, such as this one of his own dog, are powerful and have both intellectual as well as artistic strength. Bard uses layer after layer of oils to build up the feeling of enormous power.

5 Sir Edwin Landseer's "A Dog Looking out of a Kennel," oil on panel, 1837.

6 Pamela Storey Johnson did a series of dog paintings, and each had a well-known saying around the edge. In this case the pampered pug is indeed having his day. Oil on panel. A limited edition of seriographs of this image can be found.

Leisure

The categories that fall into this chapter are ones that have delighted painters and photographers for many, many years. One thinks of the ballet, and Degas comes to mind immediately; typical sporting images include going to the hunt with hounds, or baskets of fish; while food and wine bring forth a gourmet collection of images from the seventeenth and eighteenth centuries in the Low Countries and Spain. Interestingly, food and drink are, in the early years of the twenty-first century, once again becoming very popular artistic subjects. The latest trends include bowls of garlic, tromp l'oeils of fine bottles of wine, and—as always—baskets of vegetables in the market and bowls of fruit, whole and cut open.

The world of cinematic images is solely the world of photography, and there are many still photographs that instantly bring forth a memory, not only of a movie long past, but the era in which it was created.

"SALLEY. 1998."

CHATEAU
BRANE CANTENAC
1er VIN

1982

S·BROWN

3

1 "Lemons on a shelf with blossom" by Galley, oil on panel. Once again we have chosen a narrow horizontal painting—it can be seen how good this shape always looks in conjunction with other formats. Lemons are the favorite fruit in paintings.

2 "Densmore Shute Bends the Shaft," by Harold Edgerton. Most golf images are predictable but this one is so amazing that I felt it was the one and only golf photograph I wanted to illustrate since it would appeal to everyone—not just golfers. It

seems to encompass all the emotion of this addictive sport without any of the platitudes or expected vistas of Scottish golfcourses.

3 Another of David Remfry's inspired drawings for Stella McCartney. His combination of great draftsmanship and elegant sexuality reminds me of the work of Egon Schiele.

4 Stewart Brown is another artist who has perfected the art of the photo real. His oil and caseine painting on board of corks in a box is the ultimate wine buff's painting.

1 Michel Lablais' paintings of food and drink are impeccably oriental and ordered, but with a trace of humor. There is a simple understatement about his work, yet he always adds that little something that gives it international appeal. From a series entitled "Cuisine Chinoise."

2 Figs are up there with lemons as really popular fruit in paintings. Galley's oil on board gives the figs-on-a-plate painting a more modern slant yet there is still the traditional china bowl and marble ledge.

3 This fine image of hands and bread by Tessa Traeger is from her "Ardeche" series. The edition is numbered but an open edition, and the prints are on gold tone Kentmere art classic paper. This is a truly perfect bread image and would look great wherever bread is served.

4 "Asparagus" by Allan Jenkins (2000). A toned cyanotype in an edition of 18. This oversized, wonderfully printed bunch of asparagus so grabbed my attention when I drove past the gallery that I had to drive around for ages to find parking to return and discover whom it was by.

Food and Drink

Restaurants have, for many years, filled their walls with paintings. La Colombe d'Or has a wonderful collection of paintings and sculpture that the customers may see. In the early years of the twentieth century such artists as Picasso, Matisse, Léger, and Miró were to be found among the diners. They often gave paintings and sketches to the owner instead of payment, and these are dotted around the buildings together with art that the owners have continued to amass—a treat for the eyes as well as the taste buds. Other venues where such wonders exist are the Chelsea Arts Club in London; The Penzance Arts Club in Cornwall and the Comfort Art Hotel Siru in Brussels, where each room contains the work of a different contemporary artist. (Today, modern restaurants tend toward simple black-and-white photography if they have anything at all.)

Kitchens today have, in many cases, taken the place of formal dining rooms, and families spend fortunes on equipping themselves with large and wondrous eating parlors rather than kitchens per se. It is therefore not surprising that many of these eating parlors also have really interesting and well-chosen pictures on their walls.

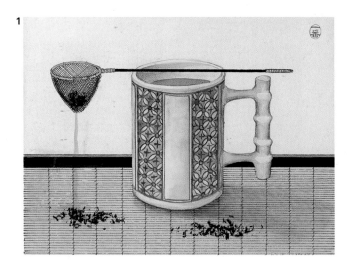

1 Large modern oil on canvas of quinces by Betty van der Voort. Van der Voort's canvases are oversized and contemporary, but are perfect with both antique and modern furnishings. I have one in my drawing room—see page 167. I did not want anything abstract or cold, and van der Voort's work is perfect.

1

A feast for the eyes

David Levin
Owner of The Capital Hotel and Restaurant

Food and art have long held court with each other, and restaurateurs have, over the years, benefitted by association with fledgling artists fed in exchange for their artwork on the walls. This happy coupling has led to some extraordinary collections housed within restaurants. The Colombe d'Or in the south of France has one of the most valuable private collections in the world. La Coupole in Paris has marble columns enhanced by the work of Chagall and Léger. It is not just the domain of the French, however. The charismatic character of Peter Langan, a man with a keen eye for art, befriended the cream of British Pop artists in the 1960s, and his restaurant, Odin's in London, boasts one of Britain's finest collections, with diners gazing up at Hockney, Proctor, Laura Knight, Gaston LaTouche, Sickert, and Edmund Dulac.

Artists now are all too aware of the impact they can play in the design of a restaurant. Designers incorporate their work into increasingly elaborate and high-tech surroundings, though not necessarily guaranteeing success!

At Pedro's in New York, the manager was telling me that people no longer come for the food but for the table. Ironic now that the table by the kitchen, once reserved for unruly or disliked customers, is now the table of choice. Customers fight to be part of the kitchen and all its drama, like Charlie Trotters in Chicago and Gordon Ramsey at the Connaught, where the best table is IN the kitchen. Bars and restaurants are opting for an open-plan style, something that I insisted on in my own restaurant over 30 years ago. In the age of the celebrity chef it is the chef that has become the artwork.

2

2 "Figs on a Plate with Plum Blossom" by Elaine Pamphilon, mixed media. Another image of figs—always fitting for an eating area or kitchen.

3 "Proportion and Harmony" by Zachary Zavislak, Cotan 2001, chromogenic print limited to an edition of 10. This is a haunting image redolent of the Bodegones of Spain—the earth paintings of food so very different to the still-life paintings of more northern European countries.

Suggested reading:

Rude Food by David Thorpe

Plant Kingdoms The Photographs of Charles Jones by Sean Sexton and Robert Flynn Johnson

3

1 "The Rockettes" by Weegee (1958). A kaleidoscope image of the Rockettes dance troupe—very Busby Berkeley and very 1940s. A somewhat atypical photograph from the master of the dark side of life.

2 Claxton has captured in this image the haunting beauty and heart-wrenching vulnerability of the wonderful Marilyn Monroe.

3 A publicity photo from the John Kobal collection. Gene Kelly of *Singing in the Rain* fame (1951). Everyone understands the *Singing in the Rain* connection, even if they have not seen the movie. Hollywood shots like this are simply the most evocative of all.

Theater, Film, Music, and Ballet

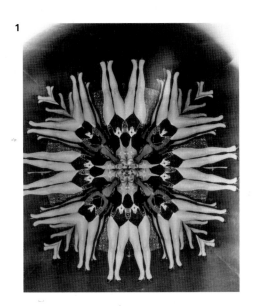

There are several artists I have met and worked with who work in the fields of both opera and theater, as well as producing equally magical paintings for the art world. This is an interesting—but not an easy—crossover. What is possible in the theater, under lights and on a stage, does not always work in a drawing room or entrance hall! I have theatrical art in my own home—and have often exhibited such work—so I feel I can write with enthusiasm about this field.

In the case of the movies we have two distinct areas: the magnificent posters that were produced in the golden age of Hollywood and indeed in the arena of French movies; and the stills that photographers such as William Claxton, Slim Aarons, and others took when, with their great artistry, they captured the moment, that essence, the character of a star. Slim Aarons recorded the world of the rich and famous from Palm Beach to Hollywood—everywhere the gilded people went, Aarons was invited and welcomed by all. He was accepted into the lives of the famous because they loved having him around *and* they knew he would always make them look good.

Film images can easily be built up into an interesting and attractive collection and make a dramatic wall or two when framed (perhaps differently) and hung well. All the photo archives have good movie stills and portraits. Rock stars and jazz musicians are a perfect subject for a collection for the same reason.

Suggested reading:

The Fugitive Gesture: Masterpieces of Dance Photography by William Ewing

Theater and Dance Photographs by Lotte Jacobi

Golden Age of Jazz by William Gottlieb

Honky Tonk by Henry Horenstein

1 I have chosen one of Paul Himmel's ballet photographs because in my eyes they are the very essence of ballet rather than images of specific dancers or ballets. Ballet is a great subject to collect, and many archives have photographs. The subject really lends itself to photography.

2 "Dinner Jazz." The legendary Louis Armstrong eating a plate of spaghetti in Rome in 1949 and photographed by the equally legendary Slim Aarons.

3 The small, still figure of Judy Garland, lit by a spotlight alone on the vast stage. Her never-to-be-forgotten voice pervades the image. An icon of song and musical comedy, she was loved as much for her weaknesses as for her talent. Her soul seeps through the page into one's heart.

4 Who would ever have thought that Abba would live forever? It is a testimony to their music that they are still today danced to by people who were not born when they were famous. One must never underestimate the power of popular music.

Dramatic displays

Yolanda Sonnabend
Portrait painter and costume designer

As both painter and designer, what I select to hang on a wall is possibly eclectic and unorthodox, without rules, but with a particular aesthetic. I place what I need to see, always in relation to the wall, large or small, or even in defiance of it. The wall supports whatever inspires me, past and present, and what goes up is variable and various. Instinctively I integrate these choices, relating shapes and colors to the proportion of the room. What may appear chaotic to the unfamiliar eye nevertheless has a harmony, an underlying synthesis, structure, and pattern that holds these disparate objects together.

I make little distinction between mediums: painting, portraiture, and design. The links are inevitably color, space, and line. If I look about me, I see random objects, a cluster of painted surreal African sculptures, plaster casts, a head of Napoleon, écorché limbs, a group of wooden spoons, cards I have collected, photographs like paintings, paintings like photographs, an Old Master juxtaposed with a spectral Indian shrine.

Collecting is a passion and I have a very minor one: votives—small, glittering church objects. There are models of heads, legs, even people forming a mysterious wall, alongside symbolic prayers aiding recovery. I group them in a narrow glass box; it hangs on the wall, but is seen indirectly. Some objects I think should be frontal, immediate, and others secretive, half hidden in recesses. Frames, of course, are vital; surrounding and containing the object, isolating the treasure. Their measure—whether narrow, wide, or balanced—gives life to the piece. Sometimes the object needs space and the frames assist in defining that space.

When I design for the theater the process is complex, a conglomeration of skills and collaboration. I have worked for the ballet (costumes and sets), where color, form, and characters come to life. The design must relate to the music and confirm the work, and I believe that theater has helped me as a portrait painter. In portrait work, character, texture, shadow and light, the pose, the search, the contact with another human being come to life as in theater, but enduringly so. Disparate elements (such as architecture, sound, and structure) also play their part. As in the theater the actor leaves, the curtain falls, and one is back to one's own odyssey and dreams.

I suppose, as an artist, I produce my own personal gallery and believe most people are visual or can be taught to think visually. And I would encourage them to hang whatever pleases, excites, or placates them, regardless of fashion. I make no distinction between art forms and so will hang whatever interests me. If it no longer remains on the wall, its magic has passed, but the work that remains becomes an everlasting talisman!

Fashion

One only has to look at the prospectus of shows for any decorative-art museum to see that fashion is now virtually indivisible from art. There are hugely successful fashion exhibitions at the Victoria and Albert Museum in London, as well as the Metropolitan Museum of New York. Philadelphia is about to launch a Schiaparelli show, and Manolo Blahnik's recent exhibition of shoe designs was a total wow.

Costume—both historical and for theater, ballet, and opera—has always been within the province of art history and is still very important to historians, fashion writers, and students of the various performing arts. Today, in addition to costume exhibitions, there are wonderful shows of contemporary fashion. Mainstream museums—and new galleries like the Zandra Rhodes Fashion Museum—are all venues for fashion as art.

On a recent visit to the Savannah College of Art and Design in Georgia, I noticed several of the graduates had excelled in a wonderful hybrid art form of part-art, part-fashion that I found totally mesmerizing. Such artists as Amanda Leibee and Jamee Linton came to mind. Rebecca Hossack (in London) shows several such artists in her West End galleries, and we, too, in Walton Street achieved great success with the "ghostly dresses" of Jimmy Stephen-Cran of Glasgow.

The graphite drawings that David Remfry was commissioned to do for Stella McCartney's promotional campaign were subsequently exhibited (again at the Victoria and Albert Museum), and this introduced yet another layer to the art of fashion.

3 "Rogue Trader" is the, no doubt, apt title of this three-dimensional white suit by Jane Goodwin (2002). The suit has a metal frame and is mixed media—fabric and acrylic paint. Another great example of twenty-first-century three-dimensional art.

4 "12 Dresses" by Amanda Leibee, photographed by Chia Chiung Chong. Looking like the spirits of children, the dresses are made from tracing paper, thread, and wire, and hung on special hangers. An ethereal and atmospheric work that could add great feeling to a room.

5 "Les Apparitions" by Nancy Wilson-Pajic. One of a collection made in collaboration with haute couture designer Christian Lacroix. Each photogram is a life-size rendition of an item by Lacroix. This process gives an intense blue image that is exciting, dramatic, and beautiful.

6 Gordon Chandler's metal kimono is the sort of exciting three-dimensional part-picture, part-object that I find a perfect acquisition when buying art. This particular one is dramatic, inventive, and very cool.

5

6

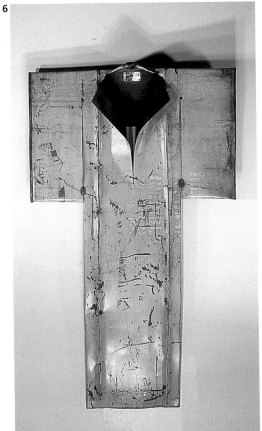

1

1 From a collection of original watercolors depicting the shoes in the collection of the Saxony royal family, housed in the Staatliche Kunstsammlungen, Dresden. It dates from the eighteenth century, but looks remarkably like twenty-first century Prada!

2 Jamee Linton's three-dimensional dress is entitled "Elizabeth" (2002). There is a tremendous vogue for fashion-oriented art to be hung without frame or stricture and to move. This is exciting in a contemporary or a traditional surrounding.

2

Fashion in art

Marie Aja-Herrera
Professor of Fashion, the Savannah College of Art and Design

The relationship between art and fashion can be said to reflect a juxtaposition of ideals, trends, and the *zeitgeist*—the spirit of the time in which a particular piece of artwork was produced.

During the latter part of the nineteenth century, with the growth of experimentation and exploration in the arts and sciences, together with the development of an affluent middle class, fashion began undergoing major changes approximately every 20 years. As disposable income grew, society was able to follow styles that changed ever more quickly. At the same time, artists began using the then-new technology of photography as a means to experiment creatively.

This type of exploration has continued in the twentieth and twenty-first centuries with the use of new technologies such as digital imaging, video, and film to create a mood or representation of fashion and clothing in art. Drawing, painting, and sculpture are no longer the only means of representing the human image.

In recent decades, two dominant trends have emerged. One is the growing youth culture, which desires above all to be set apart from the mainstream. This trend has led to the development of multiple fashion subcultures and street styles, fashion statements that often fuse ideological and cultural concepts. In another development, designers and artists working within the fashion industry have begun testing the boundaries that have traditionally separated art from fashion. For example, some have incorporated such complicated intellectual concepts as deconstruction theories into their designs; others have made use of materials not usually associated with clothing at all, such as fiber-optics. An even more extreme example of this amalgamation of fashion and art is the concept of clothing as wearable art. Artists working in this area use such techniques as painting on cloth to produce an art piece that is at the same time functional.

Fashion and fashion in art reflect the dual elements of societal acceptance and rejection, thereby forming a true representation of shifting societal trends and moods. And, perhaps most important, fashion allows for the expression of individuality by responding to the creative impulse and representing the artistic spirit.

3

3 Lillian Bassman's photography is the essence of the elegance that was the '50s. Her work for *Harper's Bazaar*, of which this is an example, of blurred silhouettes and unusual compositions, was as extraordinary then as it is now.

4 "Red Bow" by Hee Jin Kang (2002). While there is much in her work that pays homage to her Korean heritage, Kang is also obviously influenced by having grown up in New York. Kang fuses together fantasy and reality in her work.

5 "Issey Miyake" by Sarah Moon (1992) from 'Coincidences.' Sarah Moon's photography is internationally renowned. Her pictures are sensuous, romantic, and very feminine. There is a softness and special dusky light that makes her work instantly recognizable and desirable.

Suggested reading:

Appearances: Fashion Photography Since 1945 by Martin Harrison

Inventive Paris Clothes 1909–1939 by Irving Penn

Manolo Blahnik: Drawings by Manolo Blahnik

4

5

1 "Homeward Bound" by Archibald Dunbar McIntosh, acrylic on board. This painting of sailing ships makes a complete contrast to photographic sports images.

2 "Ice Hockey" by Diana Palaci, oil on board. The intense masculine energy of Palaci's series on sports fascinated me when I saw them in the Hotel Residencia in Mallorca. Each room had a painting by a different artist, and each had been given a different energy in this way.

Sports

Traditionally, paintings of horses and horse racing, as well as the ubiquitous paintings and prints of fox hunting, have always graced the walls of large—and even not so large—homes. Today in the homes of baby boomers, sporting pictures tend to be black-and-white photographs of a moment in a grand-prix event or when a favorite team won the league.

Warwick Woodhouse of Getty Images says that one of the most popular sports images held in the archive is a panorama of Stamford Bridge soccer stadium taken by A. H. Robinson in 1920. "The glass plate negative this image was taken from enables the enlargement of the photograph to a degree that an enormous amount of detail can be seen. The picture ceases to be a record of a football ground (soccer field) but becomes a wonderful window into a social world where every inch has some activity going on. In fact one's eyes are not drawn to the players, but the crowd and the activities going on around the ground."

3 Stamford Bridge soccer stadium, London, photographed in the very early twentieth century. This is the most popular leisure photograph in the Getty archive.

4 "Untitled #7, Cascais, Portugal" from the series "Swimming Pool" by Karine Laval (2002). This photograph has a narrative quality about it—somehow it seems a more intellectual image than the others we have chosen here.

4

Sports photography

Warwick Woodhouse
Senior Vice President, Getty Images

Sport, in any setting, lends itself to the camera. Sport is the great leveler and can evoke the most extreme emotions in almost any culture. It is truly international. The camera captures and distills the power, rhythm, drama, and character down to a single moment. Photographers of sports thrive on the emotion of their subject.

Sports photography is not confined to posters or clippings hastily pasted on doors. The passion of a child with an image of a favorite sports icon, perhaps torn from a magazine, grows with age and is translated into the beauty and quality of a high-end photographic print.

If one looks at a sports image purely as a shot capturing a favorite team or an individual, the true value of the image will often be lost. The visual image can evoke a range of emotions, and with sports imagery, the simple image can represent teamwork, drive, speed, power, precision, control, commitment, courage—even humor.

There is absolutely a place in our homes for sports photography, and the quality of the image and craft of the photographer remain unquestioned.

Framing

1

2

Previous page: A collection of Southern photographs, all framed simply, in Tim Hobby's apartment. They are by Roberto Rincon; Frank Yamrus; Annie Langon; an unknown photographer; and Chris Verene.

1 A fascinating multiple-image photograph by Noel Myles has been framed in the look of antique crocodile, but it is in fact ostrich; a luxury edge for framing.

2 This silver frame is made of very fine sheets of pure silver wrapped around a wooden molding and held in place with tiny nails. This is costly to make as it is labor intensive. The effect is worth it: supremely elegant yet simple. Image by Ron Van Dongen.

3

4

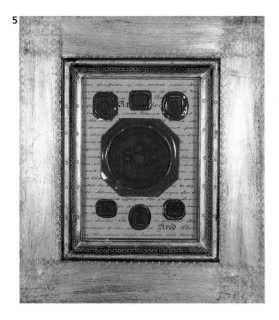

5

Matching Picture to Frame

There is no more difficult decision to make than which frame to use on your painting or photograph—so do not think you are alone in the world when you struggle to make this sort of choice. A good frame can enhance an image enormously, and a bad one often totally ruins the effect. This means that so often one plays safe, and the result—although not disastrous—can often be boring and non picture-enhancing.

As a rule of thumb, I believe that a very large painting often looks best with a very slim, almost imperceptible, frame—a silver, golden, or wooden "edge" that simply finishes off the folded canvas. A really small painting, however, can look amazing when totally "overframed" with a very large and elaborate frame. This has the effect of making the tiny picture look extra precious.

If you are framing a series or set of prints, paintings, or photographs to be hung together in an orderly fashion, I believe that the frames should be simple as too many elaborate identical frames can look over-fussy and detract from the art.

Find a framer you can trust and, most important, someone with taste that you like—if you like what he has done for other people or what you see in his framing shop, for example. Spend time playing with the different corner samples around your painting or photograph to try to get an idea of how the framed work would look—this is not a failsafe method of success, but it will at least give you an idea.

When choosing the mat for your picture, think about leaving space around your painting or photograph to give it space to breathe. This can be done with one of the new gesso mats; with a traditional mat or, better still, by "floating" the paper or canvas, showing the edges. This looks particularly good in the case of a drawing done on handmade paper where the edges are rough and thready.

3 The watercolor of a slender palm tree has been aptly framed in a combination of gesso, gold leaf, and bamboo, giving the tropical painting a tropical feel. It is always important to frame the painting to give it life, space, and meaning, and Antonio Scialo has done this here. We framed a whole collection of palm trees this way for a conservatory in Florida.

4 One of the images framed by Michael Houghton for Marco Pierre White. The juxtaposition of shapes, close together,

is used to striking effect. Here a rectangular image is displayed in an oval wooden frame.

5 This wide, simple distressed gold-leaf frame with elegant inner edge was devised by Chris Egerton as a perfect frame for collections of intaglio and wax seals. It is equally at home in both traditional and contemporary homes, though I personally prefer silver to gold in contemporary settings.

Traditional Framing

1 A small gold frame is still the most universal method of framing. It says good quality and good taste.

2 An eighteenth-century drawing, of an architectural element framed in black gesso with gold leaf.

3 This eighteenth-century print has been framed in a strong, wide black lacquered frame with an edge so the frame does not meet the dark print.

4 This enchanting French oriental watercolor was framed in a distressed gilded frame so as not to overpower it.

5 Here I have used an antique frame that I found after I bought this eighteenth-century drawing.

6 Andrew McIntosh Patrick of The Fine Art Society shows that a wall of totally different frame styles can look fabulous hung together.

On framing

Norman Blackburn
Antique framing expert

How satisfying to re-create an antique object that may have seen better days. With the very many and varied sources—auction rooms, "auntie," or attic—from whence you may acquire an old print, there is every possibility that one or all of its components will need attention. The engraving may be damaged, which will require the help of a paper restorer, or the frame may be so badly woodwormed that it is beyond further use, in which case a replacement is needed. Here your staying powers will be well and truly tested. There are a small number of period frame suppliers who will be able to advise.

The number of Hogarth prints available in the eighteenth century fostered the famous "Hogarth frame," which at its inception was a pine or fruitwood frame with hand-carved gilded decoration on the inner and outer edges. One has to accept that to match an authentic eighteenth-century frame to an eighteenth-century engraving may not always prove possible, and a sympathetic nineteenth-century frame may solve the problem. (At all costs avoid the worst of the present-day, inferior Hogarth design, which gives the appearance of a shiny plastic finish.)

The introduction of more varied print-making techniques in the mid-nineteenth century saw a further diversification into the use of veneered rosewood and maple wood finishes giving their warm glowing colors. With diligence these frames can still be acquired, and I would encourage patience in endeavoring to find them. However if you have a set of four, six, or more prints, due to the passage of time finding sets of period frames is almost impossible. Your only recourse here is to have a reproduction set made as close as possible to the original style.

Period houses and furniture are dramatically enhanced by the addition of sympathetically framed old engravings. If the self-help road is really too daunting, contact a dealer, and their knowledge coupled with your own good sense will be naturally rewarding.

1 Here is an example of using a large, wide, ornate frame with a small, simple, hand-colored engraving. I really find this brings out the best in a tiny picture. It is possibly unusual to overframe in this way but be brave. Try it and you will be very pleased with the result.

2 Stephanie Reeves has hung a wall with a series of black-and-white engravings in two different shapes. She used a fine black-and-gold frame style that works well without being conventional. With black-and-white engravings, try to find a slightly wider, more striking frame.

3 This is virtually the same frame as that on page 125 containing wax seals. It is also designed by Egerton, and with the addition of gold scrollwork at the corners, it makes a perfect frame for a nineteenth-century san-guine engraving of angels.

4 The really minute watercolor of an Indian palace has been laid down on a gessoed mat and then framed in cream gesso with a gold inner rim. I like using gold inner rims on frames—they give added life to paintings. This method could be considered "over-framing," but it really works.

Gilding

Antonio Scialo
Master gilder and framer

I was apprenticed to the great Italian gilder, Remo Constantini, where I learned the art of gilding. I then went on to master gilding techniques by working with Ghibello, a great gilder and framer who worked in London, and whose work was well known and much admired.

I prefer to work only in water gilding. This original method—a beautiful one—is the best of all gilding. The gold leaf is applied with water, but it is the technique rather than the materials that are important. It is all about time, preparation, gessoing, using rabbit-skin glue—there are no short-cuts in obtaining the perfect finish. (Oil gilding is quicker and, so, less costly, but I do not like to use it because the quality and finish are quite different from water gilding.)

There are also many machine-gilded frames today and—although excellent—the difference between a frame that has been machine-gilded and one that has been made by hand is enormous. The corners never have the same, even finish, and somehow the overall luster and variations are not nearly as subtle. Fine hand-made gilded framing is very labor intensive—and therefore costly—but nothing can ever be as wonderful as a made-to-measure specifically designed frame.

Framing Photography

2 In Wheelers restaurant, Marco Pierre White commissioned Michael Houghton to frame a collection of black-and-white photography from Getty Images in many different shapes and sizes. This combination of circles and rectangles has become the signature of this newly styled traditional restaurant.

3 This photograph by McDermott and McGough is framed in a wide black frame. Black on black used with discretion is very strong.

4 In Anne and Forbes Singer's penthouse their traditional furniture serves as a perfect foil for a modern photograph simply framed.

Framing photographs

Steve Ball

Made-to-measure framer

The big change in framing photography seems to have taken place around 1993. Pre-1993 all photography seemed to be framed in off-white acid-free mat board with a narrow black wooden frame. After 1993 anything and everything became possible. There have been some excesses, but in the main the change has been a good one.

Today, photography as art is very much a concern, so framing has become much more important. It is in vogue and can be seen everywhere at every level. The frame must be very carefully thought out—it must never "take over" the picture. It should augment, it should complement, it should suit the picture. It should be tailored, like a custommade garment, to act as the perfect frame for the particular image. You should also consider where the photograph will be displayed; this is important in the choosing of a frame.

The personality of the owner is another factor to take into account—everyone has their own sense of style and the frame should complement this. I have even found that at different times in their lives people want a different emphasis.

It is essential to use acid-free mat board to mount the photograph. I think everyone knows this, but what is not as well known is that one must also use acid-free fixtures to hold the board, such as special tape (preferably water-soluble so it is easily removable). The backing board should also be acid free—in fact, nothing that touches the photograph should have any acidic content. Acid-free material is often called "museum quality."

Technology has changed remarkably, and with the advent of many sorts of UV-filtered glass, it is no longer necessary to risk fading in sunlight. One can obtain UV-filtered museum glass and UV-filtered non-reflective glass; both are highly recommended for good photography.

There are many different materials that can be used to frame photography. Wood

is a natural choice, and almost anything can be done with it; it can be used very narrow or very wide; it can be carved and shaped; it can be painted; it can be gessoed or ornamented. Wood is, in fact, a blank canvas; the possibilities are endless.

Metals include polished steel, aluminum, rusty metal, copper with rivets, real silver … any of these are wonderfully effective with modern photography. Leather in all its forms is a good framing material. It can be found in endless colors from psychedelic to natural. It can be finished in an antique or a modern style and can be ornamented with rivets, studs, buttons, and metal straps as well as raised leather spines. Bevelled glass and lucite are very fashionable for frames, especially for portraits of the 1920s and 1930s. I have used stone and slate, corrugated cardboard, and paper. I recently found a pair of gray lizard-skin slacks that made a pair of magnificent frames!

And, finally, always dust frames with a soft duster only. Do not use cleaning materials on them.

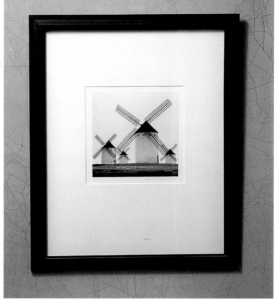

1 Chantal Fabres has placed three wonderful nudes all framed (by Steve Ball) to the picture rather than the room, using three totally different frames to make them stand out individually. Left is by Louise Dahl-Wolfe, top right by Ruth Bernard, and bottom right by Ellen Auerbach.

2 Against the rich red wall in the Firehouse, the mixture of different subjects, sizes and frame styles makes for a fascinating display. Note how good the black-and-white photography looks against a dark rich color.

3 "Windmill" by Michael Kenna, an American photographer, in the Siegel collection. The very wide mat sets it off well. Often matting is too tight, and the atmosphere is lost.

4 A large image, further enlarged to take up all the space available within a molding, is very dramatic and arresting, particularly when the image is by Bob Carlos Clarke.

Modern Framing

Trends in framing

Robyn Pocker
Expert New York framer

With three generations' experience in the framing business—and over 65 years' between myself and my brother—I can say that, aside from the vast improvements in conservation and computerization of certain processes, little has changed in the rules of good framing.

Proportions and styles still come down to the fundamentals: a good frame should enhance the art and not draw attention to itself; attention to details, such as the correct historical period, should be matched in the frame; subtle hints of colors within the picture should be brought out within the framing. These tricks of the framer's trade all serve to remind the collector that professional picture framers provide a skill that requires years to hone. The average collector may frame a couple of dozen pictures in a lifetime, while the professional picture framer is faced with hundreds of unique pieces every week, giving an unmatched breadth of experience.

Framing is still a luxury, so when people spend that money, they want real style, not an almost. The customer who walks into a custom frame shop should not be overwhelmed. A shop with a wide array of styles is only useful if the salesperson knows how to suggest the correct style and proportion. "I'll know when I see it" is never the correct approach. A good framer won't let you make a mistake in terms of technical issues or style.

2

1 Having one large, virtually unframed painting with a very simple image is the most effective way I know of changing the look of a traditional room. Nina Campbell has done this with this fine painting by Patrice Lombardi.

2 The art that Anne and Forbes Singer have chosen has given their home a very contemporary feel. The striking triptych is by Blanca Macnuca.

3 Louise Bradley has used one of Sandrine Bihorel's large works in rich reds in this contemporary setting. Here there is no frame at all—the painting is simply folded over.

1

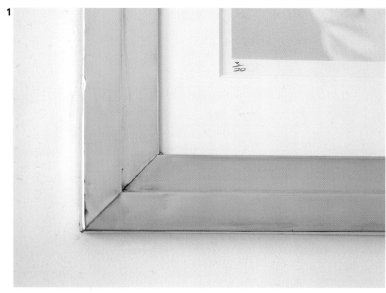

2

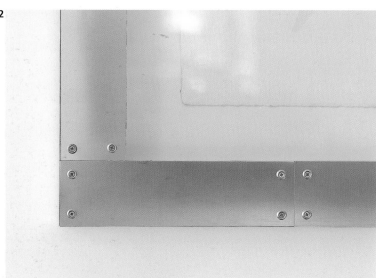

3

4

1 A "step" frame (two levels of the same material) gives an extremely elegant feel, particularly to matted art. Almost any material can be used this way as long as the frame is hand finished to give an even, seamless effect.

2 and 3 Rivets and nails can be used in a frame as extra forms of decoration rather than being hidden by paint, finished to give a very successful almost "industrial" feel.

4 A metal frame holds two pieces of glass so the image seems to float between them: a perfect way to frame these strong engravings of zebras. With contemporary styling, silver or silver-colored metals are more successful than gold.

5 Two of Noel Myles' multiple-image photographs in Chantal Fabres' living room are held simply with spring clips that allow them to float free in a simple box frame.

Conservation and Care

I think that the most important advice one can give about care and conservation of pictures is that if you feel anything has to be done to your painting, photograph, drawing, or print—please take it to an expert. Do not try to experiment yourself as you may well do well-meaning but irreversible damage. Michael Brookstone of Julian Simon Fine Art, London, gives as his first rule, "Never attempt to clean your own painting." He also recommends never to hang watercolors in direct sunlight.

With regard to photography, Michael Hoppen warns of the dangers of heat and humidity, such as radiators and fires. This applies to everything you own, particularly in the United States with its extremes of temperatures. W. Graham Arader III says that the enemies of antique maps and prints are mold, ultraviolet light, and humidity. (He suggests using UV-filtered plexiglass to control humidity.)

Hoppen says that glass cleaner should never be used—the ammonia in the cleaner builds up and can harm the work inside the glass.

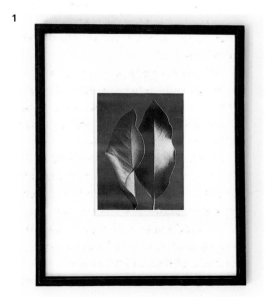

1 Mat board for silver gelatin prints, such as this vintage print, should be a buffered 100 percent rag. Overmat should always be at least a 4-ply thickness to separate photograph and glazing. This image is "Two Leaves" by Ruth Bernhard from Sarah Morthland's collection.

2 Morthland recommends sealing frames with a non-invasive material to keep out dust and bugs. This is particularly important with turn-of-the-century prints, such as these: "Daredevil Diving from Pole," "Balloonist," "Early Aviator," and "Miss French's Lightning Storm" (all by anonymous photographers).

Appraising and curating

Sarah Morthland
Fine photography dealer and curator

Remember that, as a collector, art is only with you temporarily. It will continue on its way and eventually go to other collectors. Knowing how to maintain the collection is as important as researching the art work. One has a responsibility as a collector to care for pictures. Works on paper are very vulnerable to environmental factors.

When you seal a picture into a frame, an environment is created behind the glass, so every material that is a component of that frame must be appropriate in terms of preservation. Museum-quality, acid-free materials should be used at all times when dealing with art—nothing with acidity in it should ever come into contact with the picture.

Even the best framers may not be completely up to date on current recommended framing procedures for works on paper, so talk to your framer and dealer, and research this.

Additional support in terms of maintaining your collection includes having periodic inspections and appraisals—both for insurance purposes and for an update on the condition of each piece.

I am often required to un-frame photographs that have been in collections for years. It is not uncommon to find, much to the dismay of the collector, that the framer has done something irreversible. Enlisting professional help can avert a multitude of disappointments when investing one's time and resources in art.

Displaying

How to Hang

To be a good picture hanger requires not only a great deal of experience and skill, but also a good aesthetic sense: the ability to understand which pictures look good together—and which look wonderful alone. Anyone who works with pictures and walls will have their favorite picture hanger. It is a sound investment to employ a good one, particularly when you move home or redecorate, as he or she can safeguard the condition of your pristine new walls and give you a new enjoyment of your art.

To become proficient yourself takes a great deal of practice. Use the advice given by Michael Houghton and Roddie Harris as your textbook. I have tried to illustrate different styles in hanging pictures in this book and hope that you will find inspiration in these. The choices are endless, but the mechanics and the measuring are essential.

Previous page: Fay Gold's vast experience as a dealer in contemporary art is apparent throughout her home. Each object is placed in the perfect spot, and the juxtaposition is always perfect. The statue of a horse is by Deborah Butterfield, and the large oil is by Radcliffe Bailey.

1 If a window existed where the Paul Wolfe image of the Hayden Planetarium hangs, one would have seen the same view of the building. (The Siegels' residence is directly across from the plan-etarium.) The original image was taken in 1936. The Wolfe is flanked by two Irving Penn photographs on the right and images by Michal Rovner on the left.

2 Chantal Fabres has displayed three photographs vertically on a narrow wall. This is an excellent way to hang pictures as it concentrates attention on them. Note that Fabres has not used the largest at the base and the smallest at the top, which is the more conventional way of hanging vertically.

Planning a wall

Roddie Harris
Picture hanger and designer

A focal point on a wall—particularly if you are planning on hanging a group of pictures—is essential. For me a mirror, such as a starburst or Irish bullet mirror, works best, especially if the grouping is of small pictures. If, however, you have no such feature to use, create your own by cleverly arranging the smallest of the pictures or perhaps a mixture of pictures and objects as the focal point. (When hanging a group of small pictures, keep your spacing tight.) The "weight" of a group can be at the higher rather than the lower level, by which I mean you can taper down as well as up.

The level at which you should hang pictures depends on the space you wish to fill, but as a general rule, eye-level or below is best. If you are hanging small pictures, even lower is better for visibility. Always hang pictures on two hooks placed as far apart as possible to distribute the weight evenly and to keep the pictures straight.

When hanging pictures over a sofa or chest, keep them close enough to the item to retain good visual contact. The picture will not look good if it seems to float above the object—it needs to be grounded.

When planning an entire wall of pictures, find the center and work from there out, hanging one to the left and another to the right until the wall is done. I advise using a bank of horizontal pictures in the center.

1 Jackye Lanham has hung a collection of eighteenth-century watercolors of fungi from floor to ceiling in her cool, elegant bedroom: a perfect way to use a tall narrow wall.

2 Janis Aldridge has used a combination of Basil Besler botanical engravings from the seventeenth century with small botanical engravings and a large Aubusson water-color design for a small settee.

Hints on hanging

Michael Houghton
Specialist picture hanger

Always get someone to hold the picture up against the wall for you to gauge the correct height at which to hang it. Most people tend to hang pictures too high, and you can gauge this correctly only when someone else is holding the picture. Mark the frame at the top and measure down to where the wire hangs to gauge the correct position to put in the nail.

Always put nails and screws into the wall at an angle so that the wall bears the weight of the picture, not the nail. I use hardened picture nails, not hooks.

For larger and heavier items, use chains secured to the wall with screws. Pictures need 'J' plates or hooks fixed to the back, which hook onto the chains. If you have plasterboard walls, always seek professional help in hanging heavy things.

I use a carpenter's level to hang pictures in old houses as the walls are never exactly straight. Adjust the level by eye when hanging pictures over a mantle. It *is* possible to work everything out mathematically, but the eye is most important in regulating how to hang pictures. When hanging a picture, you can use adhesive tack to keep it steady, but this will tear wallpaper, so use it with care.

If you are hanging a collection of pictures, lay them out on the floor first and draw a sketch so you don't forget the layout. Keep the outside edge even so that the collection appears as one picture. Regulate the amount of space between the individual pictures by eye.

Choosing Themes

I personally find using a theme in a room—or in a particular area of a room—a very exciting and attractive way to hang pictures. It is not, however, essential; it is purely a matter of choice.

If you are an amateur and feel totally adrift as you contemplate the naked walls in your new home, finding a theme that interests you and finding pictures or photographs that fit this theme can be an absorbing collecting hobby. To have a specific interest that you are looking for at every art fair, every flea market, on every trip around the galleries of every town you visit—this can add immense enjoyment to the collection as it grows and evolves.

I had a client many years ago who collected maps of Jerusalem. It may sound as if his collection might appear rather dull with images of the same ancient city being repeated over and over again. In fact, the depiction of Jerusalem changed with the period and the cartographer, and often depended on whether it came from a sacred or geographical standpoint. The collection was very decorative and filled the rooms with interest. One was always seeing something new and different in the collection, no matter how often one had visited.

Following a similar idea—ancient maps—Stephanie Reeves of Atlanta has used maps from all over the world, but by the same cartographer, to make a dazzling wall in her living room. Each map is of a different place but the same size and with the same framing throughout.

People collect images of frogs, rabbits, particular breeds of dogs, auriculas (one of the most popular flowers collected)—the list is never-ending. I myself collect interiors and religious paintings—how diverse are these two interests! One of the prettiest collections I ever saw was a room containing drawings, prints, watercolors, and paintings ... all of chairs. It had taken a lifetime to collect; all different sizes, styles, and periods, but dazzling.

1 On this upstairs landing, Stephanie Reeves has continued her collection of antique portraits. These are perfect with her choice of American and English period furniture and with the addition of a fine gilded mirror as a finishing touch.

2 Over her bed, Janis Aldridge has hung a selection of different flowers: paintings and prints. She has continued the theme with floral tapestry pillows on the bed.

3 Reeves has hung an interesting collection of silhouettes around a dressing room chest. These look best massed together and really give this dressing room the perfect masculine finish.

2

Caricatures relating to the same concept used to be a really easy way of building a thematic collection. It is no longer easy to amass an interesting array, but whenever I see a collection of caricatures, I am always fascinated. I have a small collection in my guest cloakroom, all relating to Napoleon.

Throughout this section, I have tried to illustrate many different ways of collecting around a theme to show how fascinating it can be, but also how important the hanging is in a collection of diverse shapes and sizes. Whatever the subject matter, it is important to find a unity when displaying a thematic collection.

3

1 This image from Fay Gold's home shows, on the far wall, a portrait of Gold by Mapplethorpe. The wallpaper in the hall is a great foil for the art. On the left are two Kara Warren pictures and on the right an Andreas Serrano.

2 Janis Aldridge has a collection of Venetian views clustered together. Paris and Venice views are much sought after, and hanging them together is a great idea. I like the casual and uncontrived way these have been hung over a toile chest.

3 In my own bedroom, this delightful group of oils and watercolors took a long time to collect. It is hard to get this look instantly, so please give it time. I think that adding the round empty frame is a perfect touch. It is an original and stylish way to finish off a group.

1 In Sarah Bredenkamp's home a large painting of a scarab-like beetle (by Bredenkamp) hangs over the fireplace flanked very cleverly by two loose ostrich skins.

2 Janis Aldridge has grouped a really exceptional collection of botanical engravings, giving an eclectic and interesting look to the room.

3 Jackye Lanham designed a great wall for Stephanie Reeves' living room. She framed and hung a series of nineteenth-century maps of countries all over the world. Note the expert placement of the pictures. I love the pair of carvings above the single maps that seem to center the arrangement.

4 In the home of Simon Wilson (of Butler and Wilson) a fabulous series of Chinese mirror pictures dominates the living room. These paintings on glass were done in China from the 1700s onward and are much collected. These twentieth-century ones look amazing hung in this way.

1 This Vernon Fisher painting on black board in Fay Gold's home makes a very dramatic statement. It is unique and exciting, and has been hung at perfect eye level. Paintings are often hung too high. **1**

Positioning

The way we hang and display our art is obviously a very subjective thing. One man's sheer delight is another man's horror, and this applies as much to the way our art is framed and displayed as the actual choice of it.

For some people the grouping of prints, paintings, and photographs is an art form in itself. When we were photographing for this book, we saw how superbly well our location designers grouped together collections of prints and watercolors, blue and white plates, clock faces, and even stoneware dishes to create inspiring walls. This is grouping at its most difficult, and attention should be given to the care they have taken to get the balance correct and to vary the ways they group from room to room and subject to subject. This is a complicated way of hanging.

Another equally difficult effect to achieve is the "eclectic wall" (see page 127). Here a collection of pictures has been framed, each to suit the picture perfectly. My advice for either of these methods of grouping pictures would be to get a professional to do it for you to save a great deal of damage to your walls.

Do not despair—there are many ways of hanging and grouping pictures that are simple and easy, which require patience, a good tape measure, and a good sense of what you want to achieve.

More and more I am seeing, in contemporary homes, a narrow shelf or plinth on which a collection of different paintings or photographs are placed (see pages 122–123 and 153). This has many advantages, the main one being that it is very easy to change both the order and the pictures displayed without any upheaval. The only permanent fixture is the shelf, so please make very sure you are putting it (or them) at the correct height. Think carefully as to where you will be when you want to look at the pictures. Standing? Sitting? Passing by? Give this decision some time; it will make a lot of difference to the effect you create, and once the shelf is in position, you are committed to displaying at this height.

2 On her staircase Chantal Fabres has hung these photographs in perfect step formation. It is important when you do this to measure carefully so that the spaces between the pictures remain constant.

3 In the same apartment Fabres has built two narrow shelves on which she has placed paintings by her children. This method makes it easy to change the art without damaging your walls.

Another interesting and very refined way of hanging is the way Sarah Morthland, a dealer in—and curator of—fine photography, has placed and hung one painting and a collection of photographs in her apartment. I find this extremely elegant in a contemporary environment.

Staircases are really fascinating areas for grouping pictures. Remember, first, that you will, in the main, be seeing them sideways on and in passing, so black and white works best. For the staircase itself, there are two basic ways of grouping pictures. You can step them up from start to finish, hanging each picture higher than the last by an equal amount. This is the conventional method and looks very stylish—particularly with a series of same-sized, same-subject images. Another way is to create a group of pictures hung together in the center of the area and leave either side blank. This way you can use any size, frame, or subject. The same methods may be used on the landings.

I am also a huge believer in the attractiveness of pictures propped over books in bookcases or in display shelves. The juxtaposition of books and objects with pictures is an interesting and arresting one (see below). A consistent color theme or perhaps a uniting subject matter can be used to draw such a collection together.

1 I love to place pictures on shelves. Here I have a wonderful collection of white glass intaglio together with two furniture maker's samples, some 1920s glass fruit, and an eighteenth-century opaline box. Above them are a large red intaglio framed and a cameo similarly framed. The items and pictures complement each other.

2 In my kitchen I have a large wall over the wine storage and use it to hang many different paintings. It seems to give the room a warm and friendly feel. In a space as large as this, placement is not easy and I suggest getting some expert help.

3 In the Siegel residence there is superb photography collected by an inspired collector, framed and hung in an exceptional way. The interesting collection of mirrors adds another dimension.

And, finally, bear in mind the environmental conditions to which you are exposing your art. Sarah Morthland warns that ultraviolet light, is very damaging to photographs. "Hanging framed photographs in as little light as possible is recommended, and the use of ultraviolet blocking glass or acrylic glazing is a must. (Acrylic has the added advantage of not shattering should the piece be accidentally dropped or knocked off the wall.) Exposure to high humidity and temperature changes is also detrimental to art, and care should be taken to hang or store works in areas that are as stable as possible." Do give these environmental factors consideration when choosing where to hang your pictures.

Using Two Walls

Always remember that walls abut walls and that it is really important to look at the whole picture. Neighboring walls need not be in any way similar, but they should balance each other so that the room has a feeling of serenity rather than the effect of walls fighting walls.

This does not mean that walls should be boringly safe in their juxtaposition, but that they should be taken into consideration—one against another—when planning what to hang where.

The example of Tim Hobby's Atlanta loft is a perfect one. On the main wall we have a large, rather brooding image that contrasts extremely well with a dark cupboard hung on the wall and filled with fine modern white china. The two walls balance well and are hung at slightly different levels. The contrast and the atmosphere are perfect, and so the two walls work together particularly well.

In the other illustration we see a totally different way of hanging two walls together. In this case Chantal Fabres has used a collection of small photographs, all framed the same, one on top of the other, to give perfect symmetry around a large bay window.

Another way of dealing with two abutting walls would be to hang one large important image alone on one wall and, on the other, to display a collection that has a theme but in many different shapes, sizes, and appearances. Again an effective contrast is achieved.

The choice is your own—the important thing is to look at the whole effect rather than each wall as a separate entity.

1 Fabres has hung a collection of small Bruce Rae photographs to "frame" a bay window. This is a very clever way of using the two narrow walls you often get surrounding a large bay.

2 In Tim Hobby's Atlanta apartment, this corner area has been superbly designed with a painting by Uri Dotan entitled "Straight" (2002) across from a modern cabinet with a collection of white china. This against the form of fine modern furniture has made the corner come alive.

Living Spaces

People assume that the living room is the room in which one most lives with—and appreciates—one's art. In many cases this is not true. Very often in the living room one is sitting with one's back to the "main" wall or, in the case of the dining room, lighting may be supplied by candles rather than electricity when one is dining. I have found that the rooms in which the maximum enjoyment is obtained from art are actually the kitchen/dining room, the entrance hall and—amazingly enough—the bathroom or powder room. It is in these rooms that one tends to get the full impact of what is on the walls more than in the "more important" rooms. The entrance area to one's home is so often forgotten—and yet this is the area first seen when one comes in, and it has enormous impact. I personally find that what I have on the walls of my bedroom is also enormously important to me.

Once again there are very many different ways of hanging and displaying art room by room, and it is really advisable to sit or stand where you will most often be when deciding on which wall to hang a particular piece or at what height. In the case of a dining room, for example, remember that you will usually be seated and that the light will not be good. In the bathroom, note what you can see while soaking in a tub or pensively brushing your teeth. By giving some thought to positioning your pictures, you will be more likely to achieve an effective display and to gain greater enjoyment from living with your art.

1 In a home designed by Jackye Lanham, a light morning room leading through to a garden has been given an interesting collection of designs framed and hung as a surround to a window. The use of the diamond-shaped frames top and bottom is a great idea.

2 Simon Wilson has had two images of faces repeated 11 times each to make this great backdrop to his settee in his living room. The balance is perfect, and he has taken great care to hang these images in exactly the right spot and at the correct height for the room.

3 In my bedroom I have a collection of religious paintings from around the world. I have grouped them together reflecting into the antique mirror. My peacock throne is by Mark Brazier Jones, and three of my grandchildren can sit in it at once.

4 Suzy Clé has hung a collection of photographs in an alcove. I love the way she has used this space for both hanging pictures and storing books. It is casual but really well planned.

1 On this fairly narrow staircase Chantal Fabres has achieved a minor miracle with really inspired hanging. She combines the use of photographs displayed on narrow shelves with those hung more conventionally.

2 The wide, grand staircase of Jackye Lanham's home has been hung with a gallery look. The antique maps fit perfectly into the moldings on the walls.

3 In Fay Gold's home a compeling photographic image by Witkin faces the descending staircase and a military row of photographs continues down the passageway.

Stairs and Connecting Spaces

These are both the most challenging and the most rewarding spaces in which to hang and display pictures. They lend themselves to what I call the "picture gallery" approach and can take numbers of paintings, photographs, or prints in many different ways.

A curving staircase presents a particular challenge. Pictures will need to be hung at different heights, and the curve can make this a tough job for the amateur. For all staircases, however, remember that one wants the pictures hung so that they can be seen from all angles, which means hanging them lower than usual.

A passageway connecting rooms presents another perfect opportunity to display a series of related works of the same size and with the same frames. It gives a good linear throughway, which is best in modern homes, but can also be spectacular in a more traditional setting.

Last, adhesive tack is invaluable for keeping pictures straight, as straightening pictures hung high on a staircase can be an hideous chore.

3

The Home as a Gallery

Throughout this book I have tried to illustrate how effective it can be to use one area of your home as a gallery—that is, to take an area like a staircase, entrance hall, or kitchen/dining room and fill it with art. This can be done in a very grand and professional way, but it can also be done by an amateur taking time, care, and a lot of effort.

Some people do this most effectively with ever-growing, ever-changing collections of photographs of family and family occasions. Others do it by collecting and displaying a collection of photographs or paintings that relate to the same subject. The subject matter and choice of hanging style is yours.

Illustrated in this chapter are three completely different ways in which a gallery effect has been created: Fay Gold has used her gym to show large and dramatic photographs by Robert Longo that are vibrant and strong, and a perfect choice for a room of action. In the Gold entrance hall we illustrate a magnificent gallery of contemporary art, while, in a high-ceilinged, stunning loft space designed by Penny Drue Baird, a spectacular and beautiful collection of aboriginal art has been hung superbly for maximum gallery effect.

For collectors of more traditional art, the apartment of Andrew McIntosh Patrick of the Fine Art Society is a lesson in living with one's art, and I recommend careful study of the way he has hung all his paintings to anyone needing guidance.

1 Two cibachrome color photographs by Sandy Skoglund illuminate the entrance hall at Fay Gold's home. They are entitled "The Cocktail Party" and "Shimmering Madness."

2 In the gym Gold has placed three Robert Longo pieces that are perfect for this great area. They are from a series entitled "Men In The Cities" (1980-81). Limited-edition lithograph.

3 In a stunning loft space designed by Penny Drue Baird, a spectacular collection of aboriginal art has been hung for maximum effect. Nothing else is required, the great canvases say it all.

Using Background Color

Using a dramatic color on walls in one's home has once again become fashionable and, more and more, we are seeing the odd room—rather than the entire home—painted in a really strong deep shade.

This is obviously a very dramatic way to change the look of a room, and much care is needed in choosing the depth of color since it is hard to gauge the strength of color and impact from a tiny sample. Try to use a very large sample in the room to gain an idea of the full effect, so that you do not achieve overkill!

A wall in a strong color offers great scope as a basis for hanging pictures. It not only totally transforms the room, but can bring the pictures alive in a way that pale walls can seldom do. A deep color can also serve to unite many different shapes and sizes of paintings and frames. In some cases a color made even deeper by the use of lacquer adds an even more intense contrast and excitement to a collection.

A deep shade of red has long been a popular color for dining rooms because it gives paintings a perfect background glow when low lighting or candlelight are used. Examples of newer colors that are seen more and more today are illustrated both in this section and throughout the book—sunny yellow in a kitchen; a dirty green in Andrew McIntosh Patrick's apartment that is perfect with his lifetime collection of paintings; a deep, almost navy blue is a dramatic choice for a dark room.

Colored walls can be a triumph to hang pictures on, but take care to look at the color in daylight and at night. Give the matter thought: too much of a good thing can be a curse rather than a blessing.

1 Amanda Eliasch has hung a large painting on the midnight blue wall of her dining room in keeping with the drama of the room.

2 The almost tobacco green color of this wall is ideal on which to hang paintings. It shows gilded frames to great advantage.

3 This tomato-red wall is an unusual choice, but with this eclectic group of paintings by Hunt Slonem and the amazing collections in the room, it proves to have been an inspired choice.

4 The yellow of this kitchen is a perfect sunshine foil to the fascinating collection of oriental and western art on the walls, from Andrew McIntosh Patrick.

5 Andrew McIntosh Patrick's collection of paintings is hung on a wonderful shade of green. It is deep and mellow, and gives a warm and very English feeling to the room while being a perfect foil for the gold frames.

Changing a Wall with Pictures

I have always said that changing a wall—or indeed a room—with pictures is a far less expensive way of redecorating than repainting the walls. Again and again, I have proved that by a simple change of what one has hanging on one's walls, one can create and achieve a totally new look room.

We recently showed the work of Betty van der Voort in my gallery in London. Van der Voort is an artist I met when I went to Belgium to interview her and photograph her home. I noticed her wonderful large and very contemporary fruit paintings, and then and there decided I wanted to exhibit them in my gallery. I had wanted to bring my drawing

5

4

1 I decided to change the main wall in my bathroom—the room in which I spend a fair amount of time! I changed the classical drawings for these wonderful paintings and limited-edition prints by the French artist Lorioz. Combined with photographs and silhouettes of my beloved grandchildren, the wall now looks quite perfect.

2 and 3 Two versions of the opposing wall in my bathroom. Note that the nineteenth-century watercolor of the golden faucet is used in each version.

2 Collections of nineteenth-century French drawings hung together with drawings of angels by Faini.

3 Drawings and a fascinating collection of watercolors of bathrooms in a vertical line.

4 and 5 My drawing room needed a change, but I didn't want an upheaval. I changed the traditional champagne bucket and glasses for seven modern eggshell porcelain vases and changed the three neoclassical pieces for one modern painting by Betty van der Voort.

room into the twenty-first century and decided to take down the neo-classical Caesar heads and laurel wreath I had on the main wall and replace them with the largest of van der Voort's fruit paintings. The metamorphosis was extraordinary, and everyone immediately commented on how much they loved my new decorations. The only change I had made was the main wall—I promise. It seems that one's eye focuses on this and nothing else in the room, and therefore the illusion is perfect.

In my bathroom, I decided to try the same easy change and added some of the wonderful rotund ladies by Lorioz to my main wall—once again achieving in an hour the effect of weeks of hard work redecorating.

The interesting thing about this sort of excursive is that changing the pictures on your walls even just from one room to another makes you far more conscious of what you display. You actually see the pictures as if for the first time. I advocate doing at least one wall a year. If you use the correct nails in the wall, the tiny holes will never show.

Picture Credits

SHG = Stephanie Hoppen Gallery

To enable you to find and purchse pictures for your home, we have given as much information on artists, photographers, owners and galleries as possible. We would be delighted to incorporate any further information if we have failed to include any relevant credits.

Page 1: from left to right: "Françoise Hardy" by Reg Lancaster, courtesy Getty Images; "Jane Birkin" by Joseph McKeown, courtesy Getty Images; "Backstage Faithfull" by Hoare, courtesy Getty Images **Page 2:** Fay Gold's home in Atlanta, oil painting by Christopher Brown, courtesy Fay Gold Gallery **Page 3:** (l to r): "Facing the Horizon VI" by Marco Crivello, courtesy the artist and the Cynthia Corbett Gallery; "Derby Spectator" courtesy Getty Images; "Watermelons" by Martin La Rosa, courtesy Praxis Art International **Pages 4–5:** Tim Hobby's apartment in Atlanta, with "Untitled 25" by Todd Murphy from the Lowe Gallery, Atlanta **Pages 6–7:** Stephanie Hoppen's apartment in London **Page 8:** 1. 19th-century drawings of cats framed, courtesy SHG 2. Tim Hobby's apartment in Atlanta **Page 9:** 3. Photograph by Amanda Eliasch in her London home **Pages 10–11:** Sarah Morthland's apartment in New York, with (l to r) "Two Leaves" by Ruth Bernhard, represented by John Stevenson Gallery, NY; "Construction" by Konrad Cramer, represented by Howard Greenberg Gallery; "Consuela Kanaga, Bodega Bay" by Imogen Cunningham, represented by Howard Greenberg Gallery and John Stevenson Gallery; "Martha's Vineyard 108" by Aaron Siskind, represented by Robert Mann Gallery, NY; Photomicrograph by Jerry Spagnoli, represented by Edwynn Houk Gallery, NY **Page 12:** 1. Chantal Fabres' apartment in London, photograph by Luis Gonzalez Palma available from Marlborough, Chile **Page 13:** 2. Fay Gold's home in Atlanta, oil by Radcliffe Bailey, courtesy Fay Gold Gallery **Page 14:** 1. Stephanie Reeves' apartment in Atlanta, pictures hung by Jackye Lanham and Roddie Harris **Page 15:** 2. Nina Campbell's apartment in London; 3. Stephanie Hoppen's apartment in London; 4 Chantal Fabres' apartment, mirror by London Metier and photograph by Luis Gonzalez Palma, available from Marlborough, Chile **Page 16:** 1. "Singing Stone" by Steve Wood, courtesy Getty Images; 2. "Empire State Building, New York 1993" by Horst Hamann, courtesy the photographer and Michael Hoppen Gallery **Page 17:** 3. "Lux" 1998, "Interior" 1998, "Interior" 1998, and "Untitled" 1998, by Marina Berio, in Tim Hobby's Atlanta apartment, courtesy the artist **Page 18:** 1. "Pyramid" by Lynn Davis and "Portrait of S.J. Perelman" by Irving Penn in Alan Siegel's New York apartment, courtesy Alan Siegel, curator Miles Barth **Page 19:** 2. Alan Siegel's New York apartment **Page 20:** 1. Photography by Kenro (centre) and Mapplethorpe (others) in Alan Siegel's New York apartment, courtesy Alan Siegel, curator Miles Bath; 2. The Firehouse in London with photographs by Getty Images **Page 21:** 3. Fay Gold's home in Atlanta, with "Moscow" by Laurie Simmons and "Figure" by Herb Ritts, courtesy Fay Gold Gallery; 4. Simon Wilson's apartment in London; 5. "Kings of Hollywood" by Slim Aarons, courtesy Getty Images **Page 22:** 1. Fay Gold's home in Atlanta, with "Dasha" and "Jasmin" by Joyce Tenneson, from Fay Gold Gallery 2. Chantal Fabres' apartment in London

Page 23: 3. Katy Barker's apartment in London, with images of Sumo wrestlers by Craig McDean, courtesy Katy Barker **Page 24:** 1. "Polyptych" by Ann Patrick in the home of Andrew McIntosh Patrick of the Fine Art Society **Page 25:** 2. Nina Campbell's London home with "White Triumphator" by Sophie Coryndon, courtesy Lucy B. Campbell Fine Art **Page 26:** 1. The London home of Andrew McIntosh Patrick of the Fine Art Society **Page 27:** 2. Katy Barker's apartment in London; 3. Fay Gold's home in Atlanta, with works by Yasumasa Morimura (top) and Sarah Charlesworth (below), courtesy Fay Gold Gallery **Page 28:** 1. Sarah Bredenkamp's apartment in London **Page 29:** 2. Fay Gold's home in Atlanta, painting by Zoe Hersey, photograph by Mike and statue by Doug Starn, courtesy Fay Gold Gallery **Page 30:** 1. Katy Barker's apartment in London, Chrysanthemum by Patricia von Ah; 2. Tim Hobby's apartment in Atlanta, with "Low Country AA# 103" by John Folsom , "Seer, Actor, Knower, Doer 21" and "Origin & Return 48" by David Shapiro, from Lowe Gallery, Atlanta **Page 31:** 3. Tim Hobby's apartment in Atlanta, with "Origin & Return 19" by David Shapiro, from Lowe Gallery, Atlanta **Page 32:** 1. "Untitled Study" by David Remfry, courtesy of the artist **Page 33:** 2. Katy Barker's apartment in London, with works by Tonio Trzebinski, drawing by Giacometti, photography by Roger Ballam **Page 34:** 1. "Study of Rabbits in sanguine" by Maria Teresa Faini, courtesy SHG; 2. Samuel H. Grimm, "Interior of Holywell Church, North Wales", courtesy Charles Plante Fine Arts **Page 35:** 3. Katy Barker's apartment in London, painting by Christopher Hill, courtesy Katy Barker **Page 36:** 1. W. Graham Arader III's apartment in New York **Page 37:** 2. Janis Aldridge's apartment in New York **Page 38:** 1. Sarah Morthland's apartment in New York, with "Apples" by Steven Bear, courtesy Sarah Morthland; 2. Penny Drue Baird room shot **Page 39:** 3. Stephanie Reeves' home in Atlanta, designed by Jackye Lanham **Page 40:** 1. Jackye Lanham's home in Atlanta; 2. Interior by Jackye Lanham **Page 41:** 3. Interior by Jackye Lanham; 4. Stephanie Reeves' apartment in Atlanta; 5. Stephanie Reeves' apartment in Atlanta; 6. Roddie Harris's apartment in Atlanta **Pages 42–3 :** Chantal Fabres' apartment in London, photograph by Luis Gonzalez Palma and collage by Samy Benmayor, both from Marlborough, Chile, and mirror by London Metier **Page 44:** 1. "Marlon Brando" by Ronny Jacques, courtesy Michael Hoppen Gallery **Page 45:** 2. "Portrait of James Joyce" by Georges Sheridan, courtesy SHG; 3. "Bibi et Denise Grey à bord du Dahu II, juillet 1926", by Jacques Henri Lartigue, courtesy Ministere de la Culture – France/AAJHL **Page 46:** 1. "Jackie Onassis" by Ted West, courtesy Getty Images; 2. "Key West Florida" 2003 by Garth Vaughan, courtesy the artist **Page 47:** 3. "Greta Garbo as Mata Hari" by Clarence Sinclair Bull, courtesy the John Kobal Found-ation/Getty Images; 4. "Steve McQueen in his Jaguar XKSS,

Mulholland Drive, 1961" by William Claxton, courtesy William Claxton Photography/Demont Photo Management/Michael Hoppen **Page 48:** 1. "Lunch on Fifth Avenue", courtesy Getty Images **Page 49:** 2. "Pablo Picasso" by Arnold Newman, courtesy Getty Images; 3. "Thoughtful Frida", courtesy Getty Images; 4. "Marilyn Monroe" by Murray Garrett, courtesy Getty Images **Page 50:** 1. "The Joker", from the series "Double Vision", 1997 by Colin Wiggins/Frank Auerbach, courtesy the artists and the Cynthia Corbett Gallery; 2. Family portrait, courtesy SHG; 3. "Portrait of a Maharajah" by E A Harris, courtesy Indar Pasricha Fine Arts; 4. "Portrait of a Young Man" by Jacob Ferdinand Voet, courtesy Julian Simon Fine Art **Page 51:** 5. "Portrait of a Child with a Puppy" by a member of the English School, courtesy Richard Philp Fine Arts **Page 52:** 1. "Old Chair" by Jennifer Anderson, courtesy MacLean Fine Art **Page 53:** 2. "Alessia with her Painting" by Armando Seijo, courtesy Thomas Corman Arts; 3. "Trisha Brown" by Joyce Tenneson, courtesy the artist and fay Gold Gallery; 4. "Hats" by Milt Kobayashi, courtesy the Catto Gallery **Page 54:** 1. "Fourteen Studies of Blue" by Jenny Thompson, courtesy Collins and Hastie Gallery; 2. "Funny Feet" by Karin Rosenthal, courtesy Akehurst Creative Management; 3. "Lips" from Humans by Henry Horenstein, courtesy Sarah Morthland Gallery **Page 55:** 4. "Jenny Torso" by Allan Jenkins, courtesy Hackelbury Fine Art **Page 56:** 1. "Nude in a Yellow Chair" by Georges Sheridan, courtesy SHG; 2. "Bordello No. 10" by Vee Speers, courtesy Akehurst Creative Management; 3. "Nude Beneath the Moon" by Suzy Bartolini, courtesy SHPA **Page 57:** 4. "Nu Horizontal" by Lorioz, courtesy Galerie Samagra/SHG **Page 58:** 1. "Jim Eicke, Bell Ranch, NM" by Martin H. M. Schreiber, courtesy Akehurst Creative Management; 2. "Coffee Bar" by Alex Dellow, courtesy Getty Images **Page 59:** 3. "Priscilla" by Joseph Szabo, "Teenage" 2003, courtesy Joseph Szabo/Michael Hoppen; 4. "Police Photo" by Weegee, courtesy Getty Images; 5. "Le Regard Oblique: La Vitrine Galerie Romi, 6ème Arrondissement, Paris" by Robert Doisneau, courtesy Atelier Robert Doisneau/Michael Hoppen Gallery **Page 60:** 1. "P.O.V." by Steven Marshall, courtesy Mark Jason Fine Arts **Page 61:** 2. "Hendaye" 1934 by Jacques Henri Lartigue, courtesy Ministere de la Culture – France/AAJHL **Page 63:** 1. "Son of the Earth" by Bea Last, courtesy SHG; 2. "The Cross, New York City, 1966/Misty Heights" by Ernst Haas, courtesy Getty Images; 3. "The Picture Gallery" by David Connell, courtesy SHG; 2. "Rio della Frescada" from Venice, a Vanishing Light (1992-3) by Sandra Russell Clark, courtesy the artist and Fay Gold Gallery **Page 64:** 1. "Pair of Gates", courtesy SHG **Page 65:** 3. "Suspension Wires", courtesy Getty Images; 4. "American International Building, New York" 1995 by Horst Hamann, courtesy the photographer and Michael Hoppen **Page 66:** 1. "Venice" by Thierry Bosquet, courtesy SHG **Page 67:** 2. "Façade of Ville de Labruguiere", courtesy SHG; 3. "Purana

Quila, Delhi" by Scott, courtesy Indar Pasricha Fine Arts **Page 68:** 1. "Bridge", courtesy SHG; 2. "Architectural Detail", courtesy SHG **Page 69:** 3. "Spiral Stairwell" by Raymond Kleboe, courtesy Getty Images **Page 70:** 1. "A Gentleman's Hall Table" by Henry Koehler, courtesy Rafael Valls Fine Arts; 2. "Cups and Saucers" by Galley, courtesy SHG **Page 71:** 3. "Le Café New Yorkais" by Anne-Françoise Couloumy, courtesy the artist and the Cynthia Corbett Gallery; 4. "Salon Huis van Loon, Amsterdam", "The Netherlands" by Alec Cobbe, courtesy Rafael Valls Fine Arts; 5. "Bedroom Interior" by Isabelle Rey, courtesy SHG **Page 72:** 1. "Chinese Chair" by Michel Lablais, courtesy SHG; 2. "Bathroom" by David Connell, courtesy SHG **Page 73:** 3. "Interior" by Thierry Bosquet, courtesy SHG; 4. "Artist's Studio" by E. de Closets, courtesy SHG **Page 74:** 1. "Paintbrushes", courtesy SHG; 2. Paintbrushes, courtesy SHG; 3. "Cutlery", courtesy SHG; 4. "Pale Vessels III" by G, courtesy SHG **Page 75:** 5. "Librario Escuela J. Mell" by Desiree Dolron, courtesy Michael Hoppen Contemporary **Page 76:** 1. "Open Dictionary 2001" by Abelardo Morell, courtesy the artist and Bonni Benrubi Gallery, NYC and Michael Hoppen **Page 77:** 2. "Design for Settle", courtesy SHG; 3. "Cinzano II" by Stewart Brown, courtesy SHG; 4. "Chair with Panama Hat and Cane" by Stewart Brown, courtesy SHG **Page 78:** 1. "Envoi de Grèce et d'Italie" by Louis Boudreault, courtesy Gallery Bourbon-Lally; 2. "Waves III" by McDermott, courtesy SHG; 3. "No. 7 from the series "Three Feet to Infinity" by Neil Reddy, courtesy Michael Hoppen Contemporary **Page 79:** 4. "Quake" by Chris Gallagher, courtesy Stephen Lacey Gallery **Page 80:** 1. "York Peppermint Pattie" from the series "See Candy" by Jonathan Lewis, courtesy the photographer and Bonni Benrubi Gallery, NYC; 2. "Yellow Earth no. 2" by Bea Last, courtesy SHG **Page 81:** 3. "Abstract in Grey" by Thierry Flon, courtesy SHG; 4. "Untitled" by Amanda Dow Thompson, courtesy Collins and Hastie Gallery **Page 83:** 1. "Beach Huts" by Jane Hewlett, courtesy Ainscough Contemporary Art; 2. "Blue Poppy" by Tessa Traeger, courtesy of the artist and Michael Hoppen Gallery; 3. "Polar Bears (Ursus Maritimus)", Hamburg 1994 by Britta Jaschinski, courtesy the artist; 4. "Sea Horse: Hippo-campus Erectus" by Henry Horenstein, courtesy the photographer and Sarah Morthland Gallery **Page 84:** 1. "Ligustrum, Bay St Louis, MS", 2000 by Sandra Russell Clark, courtesy the photographer and Fay Gold Gallery; 2. "Summer Haze, South Hams" by Stephen Brown RBA, courtesy Ainscough Contemporary Art **Page 85:** 3. "Landscape XXV: Argos" by David Parker, courtesy Michael Hoppen Gallery; 4. Ken Griffiths, "Yuma Desert 1996" by Ken Griffiths, courtesy Michael Hoppen Gallery; 5. "Farandole d'Oliviers, Mont Ventoux" by Luce Géas, courtesy Lucy B. Campbell Fine Art **Page 86:** 1. "Clouds over Yosemite" by Bob Kolbrener, courtesy Fay Gold Gallery; 2. "Facing the Horizon IV" by Marco Crivello, courtesy the artist and the Cynthia Corbett Gallery **Page 87:** 3. "Sea Fence" by Noel Myles, courtesy SHG; 4. "Summer Clouds, North End, Iona" by Sarah Carrington, courtesy Ainscough Contemporary Art **Page 88:** 1.

"Villandry, France" by Sandra Russell Clark, courtesy the photographer and Fay Gold Gallery; 2. "Isola Bella", Italy by Sandra Russell Clark, courtesy of the photographer and Fay Gold Gallery **Page 89:** 3. "Hydrangeas by the Seat" by Maureen Jordan, courtesy SHG; 4. "French Garden" by Isabelle Rey, courtesy SHG **Page 90:** 1. "Papaver Heads iii" by Penny White, courtesy of the artist; 2. "Au Jardin" by Louis Lemaire, courtesy Julian Simon Fine Art **Page 91:** 3. "Tranquility" by Zoe Hersey, courtesy Fay Gold Gallery **Page 92:** 1. "Pansies in Terracotta Pots" by Meg McCarthy, courtesy SHG; 2. "Green Cabbage in a Pot" by Meg McCarthy, courtesy SHG; 3. "Flower Engraving" by J. Weinmann, courtesy SHG; 4. "White Arums" by Galley, courtesy SHG **Page 93:** 5. Jules-Fréderic Ballavoine, "Flowers in a Pot", courtesy Julian Simon Fine Art; 6. "Spring Flowers in Pots" by Maureen Jordan, courtesy SHG **Page 94:** 1. *Fritillaria meleagris* by Ron Van Dongen, courtesy the photographer and Michael Hoppen Gallery **Page 95:** clockwise from top left, 2. *Rosa* "Black Beauty", *Rosa* "Leonidas" II, *Rosa* "Grace de Monaco", *Rosa meinivoz* "Summer's Kiss", all by Ron Van Dongen, courtesy the photographer and Michael Hoppen Gallery **Page 96:** 1. "Agave" by Ron Van Dongen, courtesy the photographer and Michael Hoppen Gallery; 2. "Iris Kaempferi (Japanese Iris)", 2001" by Judith McMillan, courtesy the photographer and Bonni Benrubi Gallery, NYC; 3. "Blushing Bride I" by Joyce Tenneson, courtesy the artist and Fay Gold Gallery **Page 97:** 4. "Parrot Tulips" by Bruce Rae, courtesy the photographer and Michael Hoppen Gallery **Page 98:** 1. "Hedgehog" by Saverio Polloni, courtesy SHG2. "The Bull" by Michael J. Austin, courtesy Jonathan Cooper Fine Art **Page 99:** 3. "Songbirds", courtesy SHG; 4. "Horse, Rider and Hounds", courtesy SHG; 5. "Tiger" by Saverio Polloni, courtesy SHG **Page 100:** 1. "Mountain Zebra III" by Jonathan Comerford, courtesy SHG; 2. "Rhinoceros (2000)" from Wild Things by Britta Jaschinski, courtesy the photographer and Eric Franck Fine Art; 3. "Brown Sea Nettle: Chrysaora fuscescens" from *Aquatics* by Henry Horenstein, courtesy the photographer and Sarah Morthland Gallery **Page 101:** 4. "Rhinoceros" by Albrecht Dürer, courtesy Christopher Mendez **Page 102:** 1. "Melba at Home, Piacenza" by Antonella Casana ; 2. "The Daily Vigil" by Barrie Barnett, courtesy William Secord Gallery **Page 103:** 3. "Oreo, Popcorn and Licorice" by Charlotte Sorré, courtesy William Secord Gallery; 4. "Mastiff Puppies" from *Canine* by Henry Horenstein, courtesy the photographer and Sarah Morthland Gallery; 5. "Boss T" by Peter Clark, courtesy of Rebecca Hossack Gallery **Page 104:** 1. "Poodle and Chauffeur" by Thurston Hopkins, courtesy Getty Images; 2. "Charlotte" by Christine Merrill, courtesy William Secord Gallery 3. "Dalmation", courtesy Getty Images **Page 105:** 4. "Ecouter la Nuit" by François Bard, courtesy Galerie Samagra; 5. "A Dog Looking out of a Kennel" by Sir Edwin Landseer, courtesy William Secord Gallery; 6. "Every Dog has its Day" by Pamela Storey Johnson, courtesy SHG **Page 107:** 1. "Lemons on a Shelf with Blossom" by Galley, courtesy SHG; 2. "Densmore Shute Bends the Shaft" by Dr Harold Edgerton,

Harold & Esther Edgerton Foundation, 2004, courtesy of Palm Press, Inc; 3. "Untitled Study" by David Remfry, courtesy of the artist; 4. "Cork Crate" by Stewart Brown, courtesy SHG **Page 108:** 1. "Cuisine Chinoise" by Michel Lablais, courtesy SHG; 2. "Figs" by Galley, courtesy SHG; 3. "Woman Holding Bread" by Tessa Traeger, courtesy the photographer and Michael Hoppen Gallery **Page 109:** 4. "Asparagus, 2000" by Allan Jenkins, courtesy Hackelbury Fine Art **Page 110:** 1. "Pears IV" by Betty van der Voort, courtesy of the artist and SHG **Page 111:** 2. "Figs on a Plate with Plum Blossom" by Elaine Pamphilon, courtesy Ainscough Contemporary Art; 3. "Proportion and Harmony, Cotan, 2001" by Zachary Zavislak, courtesy the artist and Bonni Benrubi Gallery **Page 112:** 1. "The Rockettes" by Weegee, courtesy Getty Images; 2. "Ray Charles, Marilyn Monroe, Hollywood" 1961 by William Claxton, courtesy William Claxton Photography/Demont Photo Management and Michael Hoppen Gallery **Page 113:** 3. "Gene Kelly in *Singing in the Rain*", MGM 1951, courtesy the John Kobal Foundation/Getty Images **Page 114:** 1. "Serenade" by Paul Himmel, courtesy Keith de Lellis Gallery, New York **Page 115:** 2. "Dinner Jazz" by Slim Aarons, courtesy Getty Images; 3. "Judy Garland", Las Vegas, 1961 by William Claxton, courtesy William Claxton/Demont Photo Management/Michael Hoppen; 4. "Abba", courtesy Vogue Records **Page 116:** 1. "Quant and Sassoon" by Ronald Dumont, courtesy Getty Images; 2. "Donyale Luna", Cadaques, Spain, 1966 by William Claxton, courtesy William Claxton/Demont Photo Management/Michael Hoppen; 3. "Rogue Trader" by Jane Goodwin, courtesy the artist and the Cynthia Corbett Gallery **Page 117:** 4. "Twelve Dresses" 2001 by Amanda Leibee, photographed by Chia Chiung Chong, courtesy Savannah College of Art and Design; 5. "Felicia" from "Les Apparitions" by Nancy Wilson-Pajic, courtesy the photographer and Michael Hoppen Contemporary; 6. "Green Kimono" by Gordon Chandler, courtesy Fay Gold Gallery **Page 118:** 1. "Dresden Shoes" by Gustav Buttner, courtesy SHG; 2. "Elizabeth" 2002 by Jamee Linton, photographed by Chia Chiung Chong, courtesy Savannah College of Art and Design; 3. "Mary Jane Russell", "Harper's Bazaar" 1950 by Lillian Bassman, courtesy the photographer and Howard Greenberg Gallery **Page 119:** 4. "Red Bow" 2002 by Hee Jin Kang, courtesy Michael Hoppen Contemporary; 5. "Issey Miyake" 1992 from Coincidences by Sarah Moon, courtesy Michael Hoppen Gallery **Page 120:** 1. "Homeward Bound" by Archibald Dunbar Mcintosh RSW RGI, courtesy Ainscough Contemporary Art; 2. "Ice Hockey" by Diana Palaci, courtesy SHG; 3. "Stamford Bridge" by Alfred Hind Robinson, courtesy Getty Images **Page 121:** 4. "Untitled #7" Cascais, Portugal, 2002 from the series Swimming Pool, by Karine Laval, courtesy the artist and Bonni Benrubi Gallery, NYC **Pages 122–3:** Tim Hobby's apartment in Atlanta, with photographs by Roberto Rincon, Annie Langon, Frank Yamrus and Chris Verene, courtesy Tim Hobby **Page 124:** 1. "Untitled" by Noel Myles; 2. *Cryptanthus zonatus* by Ron van Dongen, courtesy the photographer and Michael Hoppen

Gallery; 3. "Palm leaves", courtesy SHG; 4. "Derby Spectator", courtesy Getty Images **Page 125:** 5. Framed intaglio and wax seals, courtesy SHG **Page 126:** 1. Jackye Lanham's home in Atlanta; 2. "Architectural Detail", courtesy SHG; **Page 127:** 3. 18th-century print, courtesy SHG; 4. Chinese people, courtesy SHG; 5. 18th-century drawing, courtesy SHG; 6. Andrew McIntosh Patrick's apartment in London **Page 128:** 1. "Watercolour of a flower", courtesy of Janis Aldridge; 2. Stephanie Reeves' apartment in Atlanta; 3. "Drawing of Angels in Sanguine" by Maria Teresa Faini, courtesy SHG; 4. "Indian Palace", courtesy SHG; **Page 130:** 1. Chantal Fabres' apartment in London with photography by Robert Besanko, from Michael Hoppen Gallery; 2. Wheelers Restaurant in London with photographs from Getty Images framed and hung by Michael Houghton; 3. "Worn About the Neck, either for Cleanliness, Comfort, Protection or Ornament", by McDermott and McGough courtesy Alan Siegel **Page 131:** 4. Anne Singer's apartment in London **Page 132:** 1. Chantal Fabres' apartment in London, with "California Desert" by Louise Dahl-Wolfe, available from Staley-Wise Gallery, NY, Ruth Bernhard (top right) and Ellen Auerbach (bottom right), courtesy Chantal Fabres **Page 133:** 2. The Firehouse in London, with photographs by Getty Images; 3. "Windmill" by Michael Kenna, courtesy Alan Siegel; 4. The Firehouse in London, with photographs by Getty Images **Page 134:** 1. Nina Campbell's apartment in London **Page 135:** 2. Anne Singer's apartment in London; 3. Louise Bradley room shot with panel by Sandrine Bihorel-Hauquiert, courtesy SHG **Page 137:** 5.

Chantal Fabres' apartment in London, photography by Noel Myles, courtesy SHG; **Page 138:** 1. "Two Leaves" by Ruth Bernhard, represented by John Stevenson Gallery, courtesy Sarah Morthland Gallery; 2. Sarah Morthland's apartment in New York, including (clockwise from top left) "Daredevil Diving from Pole", circa 1890; "Balloonist" circa 1910; "Miss French's Lightening Storm" circa 1909; "Early Aviator" circa 1913, all anonymous **Page 140–1:** Fay Gold's home in Atlanta, with oil by Radcliffe Bailey, courtesy Fay Gold Gallery, and horse statue by Deborah Butterfield **Page 142:** 1. Alan Siegel's apartment in New York, "Hayden Planetarium" by Paul Wolfe with photographs by Irving Penn and Michal Rovner; 2. Chantal Fabres' apartment in London **Page 144:** 1. Jackye Lanham's home in Atlanta **Page 145:** 2. Janis Aldridge's apartment in New York **Page 146:** 1. Stephanie Reeves' apartment in Atlanta **Page 147:** 2. Janis Aldridge's apartment in New York; 3. Stephanie Reeves' apartment in Atlanta **Page 148:** 1. Fay Gold's home in Atlanta, with works by Kara Warren (left), photograph by Andres Serrano (right), portrait of Fay Gold by Robert Mapplethorpe (through door), courtesy Fay Gold Gallery **Page 149:** 2. Janis Aldridge's apartment in New York; 3. Stephanie Hoppen's apartment in London **Page 150:** 1. "Flyer" by Sarah Bredenkamp in her own apartment in London; 2. Janis Aldridge's apartment in New York; 3. Stephanie Reeves' apartment in Atlanta, designed by Jackye Lanham **Page 151:** 4. Simon Wilson's apartment in London, art courtesy Simon Wilson **Page 152:** 1. Fay Gold's home in Atlanta, with 'Shell Game" by Vernon Fisher, courtesy Fay Gold

Gallery **Page 153:** 2. Chantal Fabres' apartment in London, photography by Bruce Rae from Michael Hoppen Gallery; 3. Chantal Fabres' apartment in London **Page 154** 1 and 2 Stephanie Hoppen's apartment in London; 3. Alan Siegel's apartment in New York, courtesy Alan Siegel, curator Miles Bath **Page 156:** 1. Chantal Fabres' apartment in London, photography by Bruce Rae from Michael Hoppen Gallery **Page 157:** 2. Tim Hobby's apartment in Atlanta, with "Straight" by Uri Dotan from Momus Gallery **Page 158:** 1. Room designed by Jackye Lanham; 2. Simon Wilson's apartment in London, art courtesy Simon Wilson; 3. Stephanie Hoppen's apartment in London **Page 159:** 4. Suzy Clé room shot **Page 160:** 1. Chantal Fabres' apartment in London; 2. Stephanie Reeves' apartment in Atlanta, designed by Jackye Lanham **Page 161:** 3. Fay Gold's home in Atlanta, with work by Joel-Peter Witkin (l) and Edward Quigley (r), courtesy Fay Gold Gallery **Page 162:** 1. Fay Gold's home in Atlanta, with "The Cocktail Party" and "Shimmering Madness" by Sandy Skoglund, courtesy Fay Gold Gallery; 2. Fay Gold's home in Atlanta with work by Robert Longo, courtesy Fay Gold Gallery **Page 163:** 3. Room shot courtesy Penny Drue Baird **Page 164:** 1. Amanda Eliasch's apartment in London; 2. Room designed by Jackye Lanham **Page 165:** 4. and 5. Andrew McIntosh Patrick's apartment in London, art courtesy Andrew McIntosh Patrick **Page 166:** 1–5 All images Stephanie Hoppen's apartment in London with work by Lorioz, courtesy Galerie Samagra and SHG, and Betty van der Voort, courtesy SHG **Endpapers:** "Three Roses" by Bruce Rae, courtesy the photographer and Michael Hoppen Gallery.

Sources

AGENTS, ARTISTS AND GALLERIES

Ainscough Contemporary Art (Stephen Brown, Sarah Carrington, Jane Hewlett, Archibald Dunbar McIntosh, Elaine Pamphilon)
Drayton Gardens
London SW10 9QS
Tel/fax: (00 44) 20 7341 9442
art@acag.co.uk
www.acag.co.uk

Akehurst Creative Management Ltd (Karin Rosenthal, Martin Schreiber, Vee Speers)
10 Esmond Road
London NW6 7HE
Tel: (00 44) 20 7372 7434
na@nickyakehurst.com

Janis Aldridge, Inc
(C17th–C20th Furniture, Engravings and Decorative

Accessories)
6 Coffin @ Washington Street
Nantucket Island, MA 02554
Tel: 508 228 6673
Also 2900 M. Street NW
Washington, DC 20007
Tel: 202 338 7710
Fax: 202 338 5301

Arader Galleries
(Branches also in Philadelphia, San Francisco, Houston and King of Prussia)
1016 Madison Avenue
New York, NY 10021
Tel: 212 735 8811
Fax: 215 7359864
AraderGalleries@msn.com
www.aradergalleries.com

Also 29 East 72nd Street
New York, NY 10021

Bonni Benrubi Gallery
(Karine Laval, Jonathan Lewis,

Judith McMillan, Abelardo Morell, Ron van Dongen, Zachary Zavislak)
52 East 76th Street
New York, NY 10021
Tel: 212 517 3766
Fax: 212 288 7815
benrubi@bonnibenrubi.com
www.bonnibenrubi.com

Marina Berio
marina@marinaberio.info
www.marinaberio.info

Galerie Bourbon Lally (Louis Boudreault)
5180 Gatineau Avenue, Suite 157, Montreal
Quebec H3B 1L9
Tel: 514 866 1356
Fax: 514 871 1986
r.bourbon@sympatico
www.bourbonlally.com

Louise Bradley
15 Walton Street
London SW3 2HX
Tel: (00 44) 207589 1442
Fax: (00 44) 20 7589 2009
enquiries@louisebradley.co.uk
www.louisebradley.co.uk

Lucy B. Campbell Fine Art (Sophie Coryndon, Patrice Lombardi, Luce Géas)
123 Kensington Church Street
London W8 7LP
Tel: (00 44) 20 7727 2205
Fax: (00 44) 20 7229 4252
lucy@lucybcampbell.co.uk
www.lucybcampbell.com

The Catto Gallery (Kobayashi)
100 Heath Street
London NW3 1DP
Tel: (00 44) 20 7435 6660
Fax: (00 44) 20 7431 5620
art@catto.co.uk/www.catto.co.uk

William Claxton Photography
www.williamclaxton.com

Collins and Hastie Ltd
(Jenny Thompson, Amanda Dow Thompson)
5 Park Walk
London SW10 0AJ
Tel: (00 44) 20 7351 4292
Fax: (00 44) 20 7351 7929
caroline@chelseaart.co.uk
www.chelseaart.co.uk

Jonathan Cooper Fine Art
(Michael J. Austin)
Park Walk Gallery
20 Park Walk
London SW10 0AQ
Tel/fax: (00 44) 20 7351 0410
mail@jonathancooper.co.uk
www.jonathancooper.co.uk

The Cynthia Corbett Gallery
(Anne-Françoise Couloumy, Colin Wiggins, Marco Crivello, Jane Goodwin)
(By appointment only)
15 Claremont Lodge
15 The Downs
London SW20 8UA
Tel/fax: (00 44) 20 8947 6782
Mobile: 07939 085076
info@thecynthiacorbettgallery.com
www.thecynthiacorbettgallery.com

Thomas Corman Arts
(Armando Seijo)
(By appointment only)
24 Daleham Gardens
London NW3 5DA
Tel/fax: (00 44) 20 7433 1339
tca@btinternet.com
www.thomascormanarts.com

Thierry Demont Photo Management LLC
(William Claxton)
535 West 23rd Street, # S6J
New York, NY10011
thierry@demontphoto.com
www.demontphoto.com
www.williamclaxton.com

Penny Drue Baird, Dessins, LLC
787 Madison Avenue, 3rd Floor
New York, NY 10021
Tel: 212 288 3600
Fax: 212 288 0440

Donation Jacques Henri Lartigue

19, rue Réaumur
75003 Paris, France
Tel: (00 33) 1 49 96 09 90
Fax: (00 33) 1 49 96 09 91
ca.revol@lartigue.org /mdastier@lartigue.org
www.lartigue.org

Ron van Dongen
www.ronvandongen.com
(see also Michael Hoppen Gallery, Bonni Benrubi Gallery and Peter Fetterman Gallery)

Amanda Eliasch
www.amandaeliasch.com

Peter Fetterman Gallery
(Ron van Dongen)
2525 Michigan Avenue
Building A7
Santa Monica, CA 90404
Tel: 310 453 6463
Fax: 310 453 6959
pfgallery@earthlink.net

The Fine Art Society PLC
(Andrew McIntosh Patrick)
148 New Bond Street
London W1S 2JT
Tel: (00 44) 20 7629 5116
Fax: (00 44) 20 7491 9454
art@faslondon.com
www.faslondon.com

Eric Franck Gallery
(Britta Jaschinski)
7 Victoria Square
London SW1W 0QY
Tel: (00 44) 20 7630 5972
Fax: (00 44) 20 7630 6885
e.franck@btclick.com

Getty Images Gallery
Ground Floor, 3 Jubilee Place
London SW3 3TD
Tel: (00 44) 20 7376 4525
Fax: (00 44) 20 7376 4524
gallery.information@gettyimages.com
www.getty-images.com

Fay Gold Gallery
(Radcliffe Bailey, Christopher Brown, Deborah Butterfield, Gordon Chandler, Sarah Charlesworth, Sandra Russell Clark, Dan Corbin, Vernon Fisher, Zoe Hersey, Bob Kolbrener, Robert Longo, Robert Mapplethorpe, Yasumasa Morimura, Edward

Quigley, Herb Ritts, Andreas Serrano, Laura Simmons, Sandy Skoglund, Mike and Doug Starn, Joyce Tenneson, Karen Warren, Joel-Peter Witkin)
764 Miami Circle
Atlanta, GA 30324
Tel: 404 233 3843
Fax: 404 365 8633
info@faygoldgallery.com
www.faygoldgallery.com

Howard Greenberg Gallery
(Lillian Bassman, Imogen Cunningham)
41 East 57th Street
New York, NY 10022
Tel: 212 334 0010
info@howardgreenberg.com
www.howardgreenberg.com

HackelBury Fine Art Ltd
(Allan Jenkins)
4 Launceston Place
London W8 5RL
Tel: (00 44) 20 7937 8688
Fax: (00 44) 20 7937 8868
gallery@hackelbury.co.uk
www.hackelbury.co.uk

Horst Hamann – also available from Michael Hoppen Gallery
horst@horsthamann.com
www.horsthamann.com

Michael Hoppen Contemporary
(Hee Jin Kang, Nancy Wilson-Pajic, Abelardo Morell, Neil Reddy, Desiree Dolron)
3 Jubilee Place
London SW3 3TD
Tel: (00 44) 20 7352 4499
Fax: (00 44) 20 7352 3669
www.michaelhoppen-photo.com

Michael Hoppen Gallery
(Horst Hamann, Robert Besanko, Joseph Szabo, Ronny Jacques, Ken Griffiths, Bruce Rae, David Parker, Dr Harold Edgerton, Ernst Haas, William Claxton, Lillian Bassman, Robert Doisneau, Ron van Dongen, Paul Himmel, Jacques Henri Lartigue, Sarah Moon, David Parker, Tessa Traeger)
First Floor, 3 Jubilee Place
London SW3 3TD
Tel: (00 44) 20 7352 3649
Fax: (00 44) 20 7352 3669
gallery@michaelhoppen-

photo.com
www.michaelhoppen-photo.com

Stephanie Hoppen
(Suzy Bartolini, François Bard, Sandrine Bihorel-Hauquiert, David Connell, Antonella Casana, Stewart Brown, Thierry Bosquet, Thierry Flon, Jonathon Comerford, Michel Lablais, Bea Last, Noel Myles, Maureen Jordan, Meg McCarthy, McDermott, Gallery, G, Diana Palaci, Isabelle Rey, Betty van de Voort, Lorioz, Geoges Sheridan, E de Closets, J. Weinmann, Saverio Polloni, Pamela Stoery Johnson, Gustav Buttner)
17 Walton Street
London SW3 2HX
Tel: (00 44) 20 7589 3678
Fax: (00 44) 20 7584 3731
info@stephaniehoppen.com
www.stephaniehoppen.com

Henry Horenstein Photography
(see also Sarah Morthland Gallery)
info@horenstein.com
www.horenstein.com

Rebecca Hossack Gallery
(Peter Clark)
35 Windmill Street
London W1T 2JS
Tel: (00 44) 20 7436 4899
Fax: (00 44) 20 7323 3182
rebecca@r-h-g.co.uk
www.r-h-g.co.uk

Edwynn Houk Gallery
(Jerry Spagnoli)
745 5th Avenue
New York, NY 10151
Tel: 212 750 7070
info@houkgallery.com
www.houkgallery.com

Mark Jason Fine Art
(Steven Marshall)
First Floor, 71 New Bond Street
London W1S 1DE
Tel: (00 44) 20 7629 4080
Fax: (00 44) 20 7629 5111
Mobile: 07957 133994
info@jasonfinearts.com
www.jasonfinearts.com

The John Kobal Foundation
Mount Pleasant Studios
51–53 Mount Pleasant

London WC1X 0AE
Tel/fax: (00 44) 20 7278 8482
admin@johnkobal.org
www.johnkobal.org

**Stephen Lacey Gallery
(Chris Gallagher)**
One Crawford Passage
Ray Street
London EC1R 3DP
Tel: (00 44) 20 7837 5507
Fax: (00 44) 20 7837 5549
stephenlaceygallery@btclick.com
www.stephenlaceygallery.co.uk

**Jacquelynne P. Lanham Designs,
Inc**
472 East Paces Ferry Road, NE
Atlanta, GA 30305
Tel: 404 364 0472
Fax: 404 261 1792
jackye@lanhamdeesigns.com

**Keith de Lellis Gallery
(Paul Himmel)**
47 East 68th Street
New York, NY 10021
Tel: 212 327 1482
Fax: 212 327 1492
defoto@earthlink.net
www.keithdelellisgallery.com

**Lowe Gallery
(David Shapiro)**
Space A-2, 75 Bennett Street
Atlanta, GA 30309
Tel: 404 352 8114
Fax: 404 352 0564
info@lowegallery.com
www.lowegallery.com

**MacLean Fine Art
(Jennifer Anderson)**
10 Neville Street
London SW7 3AR
Tel/fax: (00 44) 20 7589 4384
Mobile: 07768 793442
info@macleanfineart.com
www.macleanfineart.com

**Robert Mann Gallery
(Aaron Siskind)**
210 11th Avenue, 10th Floor
New York, NY 10001
Tel: 212 989 7600
mail@robertmann.com
www.robertmann.com

**A.M.S. Marlborough
(Samy Benmayor, Luis Gonzalez
Palma)**
Nueva Castanera 3723

Santiago, Chile
Tel: (00 56) 2 228 8696
Fax: (00 56) 2 207 4071

**Christopher Mendez Old Master
Prints**
(By appointment only)
53 Clerkenwell Close
London EC1R 0EA
Tel/fax: (00 44) 20 7253 9699
cm@christophermendez.freeserv
e.co.uk

**Momus Gallery
(Uri Dotan)**
75 Bennett Street, D-2
Atlanta, GA 30309
Tel: 404 355 4180
Fax: 404 355 4181
info@momusgallery.com
www.momusgallery.com

**Sarah Morthland Gallery
(Henry Horenstein, Frank
Yamrus)**
511 West 25th Street, Suite 709
New York, NY 10001
Tel: 212 242 7767
Fax: 212 242 7797
www.sarahmorthlandgallery.com
info@sarahmorthlandgallery.com

Indar Pasricha Fine Arts
(South Asian Arts)
22 Connaught Street
London W2 2AF
Tel: (00 44) 20 7724 9541
Fax: (00 44) 20 7258 0493
info@indarpasrichafinearts.com
www.indarpasrichafinearts.com

Richard Philp Fine Arts
7 Ravenscourt Square
London W6 0TW
Tel: (00 44) 20 8748 5678
Fax: (00 44) 20 8748 2949
Mobile: 07850 470091
rphilp@richardphilp.com
www.richardphilp.com

Charles Plante Fine Arts
(By appointment only)
50 Gloucester Street
London SW1V 4EH
Tel: (00 44) 20 7834 3305
Fax: (00 44) 20 7828 3499
Mobile: 07798 626249
PlanteArts@aol.com
www.watercolours-drawings.com

**Praxis International Art
(Martin La Rosa)**

25 East 73rd Street, 4th Floor
New York, NY 10021
Tel: 212 772 9478
Fax: 212 772 0949
newyork@praxis-art.com
www.praxis-art.com

Also Arenales 1311
Buenos Aires
buenosaires@praxis-art.com
Tel: (00 54) 11 4813 8639

**The Press Association
(William Conran)**
292 Vauxhall Bridge Road
London SW1V 1AE
Tel: (00 44) 20 7903 7000
www.paphotos.com /
www.pa.press.net

David Remfry
www.davidremfry.com
remfrystudio@aol.com

Sandra Russell Clark
www.sandrarussellclark.com

**Galerie Samagra
(Lorioz, François Bard)**
52, rue Jacob
75006 Paris, France
Tel: (00 33) 1 42 86 86 19
Fax: (00 33) 1 42 86 13 04
gallery.samagra@wanadoo.fr
www.gallery-samagra.com

**Savannah College of Art and
Design
(Amanda Leibee, Jamee Linton,
Chia Chiung Chong)**
P. O. Box 3146
Savannah, GA 31402-3146
Tel: 912 525 5100
info@scad.edu
www.scad.edu

**William Secord Gallery, Inc
(Dog Painting, Merrill, Barnett,
Sorré)**
52 East 76th Street
New York, NY 10021
Tel: 212 249 0075
Fax: 212 288 1938
wsecord@dogpainting.com
www.dogpainting.com

**Julian Simon Fine Art Ltd
(Jules-Frederic Ballavoine, Louis
Lemaire, Jacob Ferdinand Voet)**
70 Pimlico Road
London SW1W 8LS
Tel: (00 44) 20 7730 8673 / 2519

Fax: (00 44) 20 7823 6116
jsimon@19thcenturypaintings.
com
www.19thcenturypaintings.com

**Tim Hobby at Space Modern
Design**
800 Peachtree Street NE
Atlanta, GA 30308
Tel: 404 228 4600
Fax: 404 228 4616
info@spacemodernworld.com
www.spacemodernworld.com

**Staley-Wise Gallery
(Louise Dahl-Wolfe)**
560 Broadway
New York, NY 10012
Tel: 212 966 6223
Fax: 212 966 6293
photo@staleywise.com
www.staleywise.com

**John Stevenson Gallery
(Ruth Bernhard, Consuela
Kanaga)**
338 West 23rd Street
New York, NY 10011
Tel: 212 352 0072
mail@johnstevenson-gallery.com
www.johnstevenson-gallery.com

**Studio 31 Platinum Printroom
(Max Caffell)**
The Studio
31 Coleherne Road
Chelsea
London SW10 9BS
Tel: (00 44) 20 7373 2916

Tessa Traeger (available from
Michael Hoppen)
www.tessatraeger.com

**Rafael Valls Limited
(Old Master Paintings, Henry
Koehler, Alec Cobbe)**
11 Duke Street
London SW1Y 6BN
Tel: (00 44) 20 7930 1144
Fax: (00 44) 20 7976 2589
info@rafaelvalls.demon.co.uk
www.artnet.com/rvalls.html

Also 6 Ryder Street
London SW1Y 6QB
Tel: (00 44) 20 7930 0029
Fax: (00 44) 20 7976 2589

Penny White
pennywhite@talk21.com

FRAMING AND PICTURE HANGING

Norman Blackburn
The Old Print Studio
7 Red Lion Square
Stamford
Lincolnshire PE9 2AJ
Tel/fax: (00 44) 1780 489151
Mobile: 07714 721846
oldprints@normanblackburn.com
www.normanblackburn.com

Michael Houghton
Tel: (00 44) 1462 458654
Mobile: 07771 561998

London Metier
28 Annett Road
Walton-on-Thames
Surrey KT12 2JR
Tel: 07947 251518
Fax: (00 44) 1932 228763

J. Pocker & Son
(Branches also in Bronxville, Rye, Greenwich CT, Westport CT)
135 East 63rd Street
New York
Tel: 800 443 3116
Fax: 877 762 3726
JPocker@aol.com
www.jpocker.com

Antonio Scialò
Tel: (00 44) 20 8776 8000
Mobile: 07885 094715

Arnold Wiggins & Sons
4 Bury Street
London SW1Y 6AB
Tel: (00 44) 20 7925 0195
Fax: (00 44) 20 7839 6928
info@arnoldwiggins.com
www.arnoldwiggins.com

PRINT DEALERS

Felix Rosenstiel's Widow and Son Ltd
(Photographic and contemporary images – prints)
33–35 Markham Street
Chelsea Green
London SW3 3NR
Tel: (00 44) 20 7352 3551
Fax: (00 44) 20 7351 5300
sales@felixr.com
www.felixr.com

Glasgow Print Studio
22 & 25 King Street
Glasgow G1 5QP
Tel: (00 44) 141 552 0704/1394
Fax: (00 44) 141 552 2919
gallery@gpsart.co.uk
www.gpsart.co.uk

International Fine Print Dealers Association:
Annual Print Fair (NY)
15 Gramercy Park South,
Suite 7A
New York, NY 10003
Tel: 212 674 6095
www.printfair.com

Stewart and Stewart
(Printer/Publisher of fine prints)
5571 Wing Lake Road,
Bloomfield Hills,
MI 48301-1250
Tel: 248 626 5248
Fax: 248 626 0972
fineprints@aol.com
www.StewartStewart.com

MAGAZINES

Art & Auction
edit@artandauction.com
www.artandauction.com

Art Monthly
info@artmonthly.co.uk
www.artmonthly.co.uk

ARTnews Magazine
www.artnewsonline.com

The Art Newspaper (UK)
contact@theartnewspaper.com
www.theartnewspaper.com

ArtReview
info@art-review.co.uk
www.art-review.com

Decor Magazine
(Art and framing resource)
DECOR@pfpublish.com
www.decormagazine.com

Frame Magazine
info@framemag.com
www.framemag.com

GALLERIES magazine
(Monthly listings for UK)
artefact@artefact.co.uk
www.artefact.co.uk

HotShoe
(Photography)

World Illustrated Ltd
hotshoe@photoshot.com
www.photoshot.com

Pluk magazine
(Photography in London, the UK and Europe)
photoguide@btclick.com

ART MUSEUMS

USA
The Frick Collection
1 East 70th Street
New York, NY 10021-4967
Tel: 212 288 0700
Fax: 212 628 4417
info@frick.org
www.frick.org

The Metropolitan Museum of Art
1000 Fifth Avenue at 82nd Street
New York, NY 10028-0198
Tel: 212 535 7710
www.metmuseum.org

Museum of Modern Art (MoMA)
11 West 53rd Street
www.moma.org

National Gallery of Art
National Mall
Washington DC
Tel: 202 737 4215
www.nga.gov

UK:
National Gallery
Trafalgar Square
London WC2N 5DN
Tel: (00 44) 20 7747 2885
Fax: (00 44) 20 7747 2423
information@ng-london.org.uk
www.nationalgallery.org.uk

National Gallery of Scotland
The Mound
Edinburgh EH2 2EL
Tel: (00 44) 131 624 6200
Fax: (00 44) 131 220 0917
enquiries@nationalgalleries.org
www.natgalscot.ac.uk

National Portrait Gallery
St Martin's Place
London WC2H 0HE
Tel: (00 44) 20 7306 0055
Fax: (00 44) 20 7306 0056
www.npg.org.uk

Royal Academy of Arts
Burlington House
London W1J 0BD
Tel: (00 44) 20 7300 8000
www.royalacademy.org.uk

Tate Britain
Millbank
London SW1P 4RG
Tel: (00 44) 20 7887 8000
www.tate.org.uk

Tate Modern
Bankside
London SE1 9TG
Tel: (00 44) 20 7887 8000
www.tate.org.uk

ART FAIRS

"Fairs are a great way of seeing a lot of galleries in a very short space of time: at a fair you can see 100 galleries in half a day, and each gallery will have brought along several artists' work."

WILL RAMSAY, founder of the Affordable Art Fair

Affordable Art Fair (London / New York)
www.affordableartfair.co.uk

AIPAD Photography Show
www.photoshow.com

Art Basel
www.art.ch

Art London
www.artlondon.net

Art On Paper Fair
www.artonpaper.co.uk

Frieze Art Fair
www.friezeartfair.com

International Artexpo
www.artexpos.com

ILondon Art Fair
www.londonartfair.com.uk

Tefaf Maastricht
www.tefaf.com

Works on Paper Fair
www.sanfordsmith.com/wop.htm

Acknowledgments

There are so many people who have assisted me in bringing this book into the world, and I fear that in thanking them I am going to sound like one of those Oscar-winners who go on thanking everyone, including the entire family! However, I could not let this opportunity pass without telling my friends and colleagues how much I appreciate the time and advice they have so freely given. I would like to thank all the artists, galleries, photographers, agents and contributors who gave so much of their expertise to us to make the book as full of information as it is.

Louise Garczewska at Getty Images was a pillar of strength to me from day one, and never did she or any of her colleagues make me feel I was being a nuisance with my endless quests for images. **Bonni Benrubi** – my new best friend. She and **Thom** were an endless source of information, assistance, wonderful images and lots of inspiration. Bonni introduced me to Alan Siegel and was instrumental in my being allowed to photograph his magnificent collection.

Andrew McIntosh Patrick, who opened his inspiring apartment to us and allowed us to photograph it, while giving us time, inspirational pep talks and extraordinary information. **Alan Siegel** for allowing me to visit his home and photograph his collection, and **Miles Barth** for his assistance and advice on many occasions. **Sarah Morthland**, the calmest and most soothing person I have met in years, who added a fascinating new dimension to the book. **Fay Gold**, her daughters, and her colleagues at the gallery for generously giving of their time and advice, for letting us photograph the Gold family home, and most of all for introducing us to **Irene Shepherd**, who was the very spirit of southern hospitality.

Ron Van Dongen, who was my very first interview and who was so kind to come to London and let me interview him face to face. He really inspired me. Everyone at **Raphael Valls** for their enthusiastic support at all times. **Michael Brookstone** of Julian Simons, who never lost his cheerfulness no matter how often I called him.

Jackye Lanham, **Stephanie Reeves** and **Roddie Harris**, who all worked and played with us in Atlanta, giving us endless walls to photograph and nannying us all over town. **Jennifer Brady** of Atlanta for introducing me to the talented and charming Tim Hobby. We shall never forget the wonderful time we all had together there.

I have to mention all the photographers who heeded my pleas and gave me their images to use in the book. Your enthusiasm, generosity and sensitivity will always remain with me, and I shall think of you whenever I look at this book. I thank you all from the bottom of my heart: especially **William Claxton**, **David Parker**, **Tessa Traeger**, **Sandra Russell Clark**, **William Conran**, **Henry Horenstein**, **Horst Hamann**, **Martine d'Astier** of the Association des Amis de J. H. Lartigue, **Bruce Rae**, **Joyce Tenneson** and many, many more.

Many photographers' agents and photographic archives gave us invaluable help, as did many galleries. **Nicky Akehurst**, **Ainscough Contemporary Art**, **Lucy B. Campbell**, **The Catto Gallery**, **Cynthia Corbett**, **Collins and Hastie**, **Hackel-Bury Fine Art**, **Rebecca Hossack**, **The Indar Pasricha Gallery**, **Simon Crocker** of the John Kobal Foundation.

I want to thank all the people who allowed us to photograph their homes in London, New York and Atlanta. Some I have already mentioned but I want to add a vote of thanks to **Katy Barker**, **Chantal Fabres**, **Sarah Bredenkamp** and **Nina Campbell**.

I called upon many colleagues and friends, who all helped in some way with information that was desperately needed. **Rose Kendall**, **Christopher Mendez**, **Richard Philp**, **Charles Plante**, **Min Hogg**, **Piers Gough**, **Max Caffell**, **David Remfry** and **David Schiff** were all more than generous, not to mention enthusiastic, in their assistance and contributions. So, too, were **Graham Arader**, **Janis Aldridge**, **Lucy Yeoman** and **Max Caffell** who all gave invaluable assistance as well as their fascinating introductions. Thanks to **Lillian Bassman** and **Paul Himmel**, for all their help and kindness, and for the efficiency of **Keith de Lellis** and **Thierry Demont**, you made such a difference.

Everyone at Bulfinch—**Matthew Ballast**, **Jill Cohen**, **Betty Wong** and **Michael Sand**. Your enthusiastic responses to my requests for information and assistance were heartwarming; I am very happy to be working with you. I must thank the creative team, who put the book together, in particular, my friend and publisher, **Jacqui Small**. To **Kate John**, my editorial manager, many thanks for finding the marvelous photograph of the Harley Davidson. Also to **Lisa Pettibone** for all her hard work in designing the book and **Simon Upton**, our location photographer: it was a great pleasure to work with him, even on the day when we had no light at all! Thanks too, to my portrait photographer, **Barry Lategan**, and **Michael Grey** for hair and make-up.

I must mention two people who have been the most amazing support to me through this exciting venture—**Vicki Vrint**, my editor, and **Joanna Norman**, head of research, the person who has remembered every last detail and image, and has been there day after day, helping us all. A visual memory is a rare and amazing talent and Joanna has this indeed—thank you, Jo. Vicki is the best editor I have ever worked with, never loses her cool and was always there to help with a quick response.

My son, **Michael**, was always there to help when I felt I had reached a dead end, and came up with the perfect photograph for each difficult spot. His excellent eye and encyclopedic knowledge were a boon and I could not have done without his advice. **Genny Janvrin** at the Michael Hoppen Gallery attended to all my queries and nagging without ever getting testy.

Thank you one and all. All this wonderful cooperation on both sides of the Atlantic has proved to me once and for all that when there is good will, everything is possible.

Index